To begin Lesson 1, you will need a pair of 10″ straight knitting needles, size 10, and a skein of [t] you use a light or a bright color yarn to help you see the stitches more clearly.

LESSON 1 - CASTING ON

SLIP KNOT

"The very first stitch is a slip knot. Those of you who are already 'slip knot experts' may skip this part and go on to Holding Yarn. You may wait for us there."

Step 1: Pull a 10″ length of yarn from the skein. Lay the end of the yarn on a table and make a circle over it *(Fig. 1a)*.

Fig. 1a

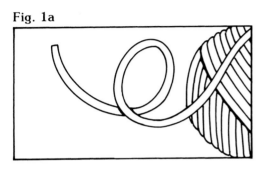

Step 2: Place the working yarn under the circle *(Fig. 1b)*.

Fig. 1b

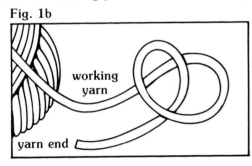

Step 3: Put a needle under the bar just made *(Fig. 1c)* and pull on both ends of the yarn to complete the slip knot *(Fig. 1d)*.

Fig. 1c

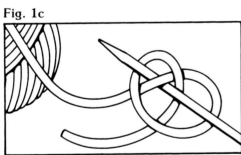

Fig. 1d

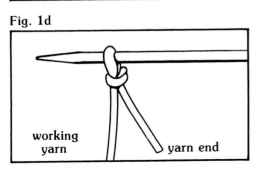

"You've done it!"

HOLDING YARN

Two methods of knitting are included - holding the working yarn in the right hand (**English Method, Fig. 2a**) or in the left hand (**Continental Method, Fig. 2b**). We encourage you to try both methods to determine which feels more comfortable. Either method will produce knitting and there is no difference in the resulting piece of work. The English Method uses the right hand more and requires less dexterity of the left hand. The Continental Method requires some dexterity of the left hand and is believed by some to be faster. Either method will be slightly awkward at first, but with practice will become easier and your work will be more even. **If you find that holding your needles or yarn in a different way is easier, by all means do it.** The important thing is to be able to control your needles and yarn, enabling you to knit and to enjoy!

Fig. 2a   **English Method**

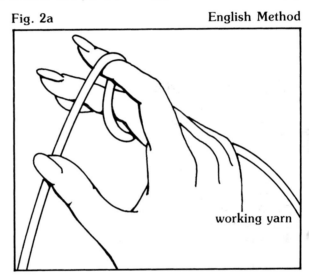

Fig. 2b   **Continental Method**

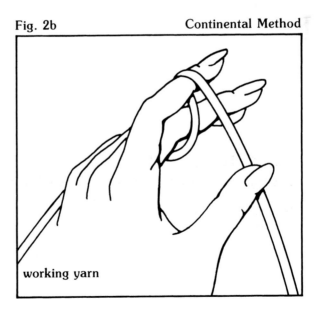

"There are several methods of casting on the first row of stitches. We're going to 'knit on' the stitches because it will make learning to knit a breeze and because someday, when you are making buttonholes or dolman sleeves, you are going to need to know this."

ENGLISH METHOD

Step 1: Hold the needle with the slip knot in your left hand. Hold the empty needle and the working yarn in your right hand. Insert the right needle into the front of the slip knot from **left** to **right** *(Photo A)*.

Photo A

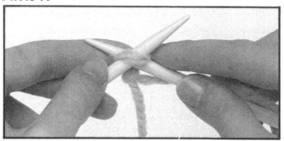

Step 2: Hold the right needle with your left thumb and index finger. With your right hand, bring the working yarn beneath the right needle and between the needles from **back** to **front** *(Photo B)*.

Photo B

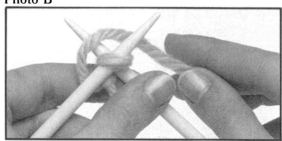

Step 3: With your right hand, bring the right needle, with the loop of yarn, toward you and through the stitch *(Photo C)*.

Photo C

Step 4: Bring the left needle forward and up into the new loop from bottom to top *(Photo D)*, allowing the right needle to slide out.

Photo D

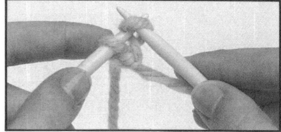

CONTINENTAL METHOD

Step 1: Hold the working yarn and the needle with the slip knot in your left hand. Hold the empty needle in your right hand. Insert the right needle into the front of the slip knot from **left** to **right** *(Photo E)*.

Photo E

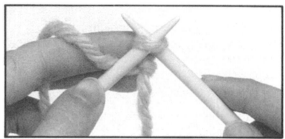

Step 2: With your index finger, bring the working yarn between the needles from **left** to **right** *(Photo F)*.

Photo F

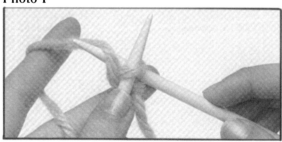

Step 3: Bring the right needle, with the loop of yarn, toward you and through the stitch *(Photo G)*.

Photo G

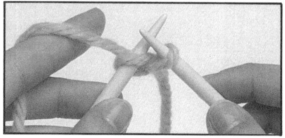

Step 4: Bring the left needle forward and up into the new loop from bottom to top *(Photo H)*, allowing the right needle to slide out.

Photo H

BOTH METHODS

It is important to slide the stitch over the tapered tip to the long needle shaft, then pull the yarn slightly (so there are no loose loops of yarn), but not too tightly because you want your cast on row to be as elastic as your knitting.

"You now have two stitches on your left needle. See, you can cast on! Now, do it again."

Repeat Steps 1-4, working into the stitch closest to the tip of the left needle, until you feel very comfortable casting on.

LESSON 2 - KNITTING

"Now pull off those three miles of stitches, leaving just the first 10 on your left needle because the big moment has arrived. You're going to knit! This is almost like casting on your stitches - but easier."

ENGLISH METHOD

Step 1: Hold the needle with the cast on stitches in your left hand and the empty needle in your right hand.

Step 2: With the yarn in **back** of the needles, insert the right needle into the front of the stitch closest to the tip of the left needle from **left** to **right**, just as you did when you were casting on **(Photo A, page 3)**.

Step 3: Hold the right needle with your left thumb and index finger while you bring the yarn beneath the right needle and between the needles from **back** to **front** **(Photo B, page 3)**.

Step 4: With your right hand, bring the right needle, with the loop of yarn, toward you and through the stitch **(Photo C, page 3)**.

Step 5: You now have a new stitch on the right needle, so slip the old stitch off the left needle **(Photo I)**.

Step 6: Tighten the new stitch on the shaft of the right needle.

CONTINENTAL METHOD

Step 1: Hold the needle with the cast on stitches in your left hand and the empty needle in your right hand.

Step 2: With the yarn in **back** of the needles, insert the right needle into the front of the stitch closest to the tip of the left needle from **left** to **right**, just as you did when you were casting on **(Photo E, page 3)**.

Step 3: With your index finger, bring the yarn between the needles from **left** to **right** **(Photo F, page 3)**.

Step 4: Bring the right needle, with the loop of yarn, toward you and through the stitch **(Photo G, page 3)**.

Step 5: You now have a new stitch on the right needle, so slip the old stitch off the left needle **(Photo J)**.

Step 6: Tighten the new stitch on the shaft of the right needle.

Photo I

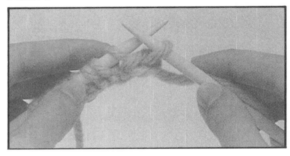

Photo J

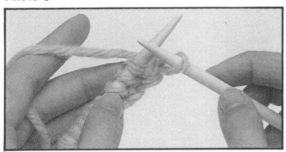

BOTH METHODS

Repeat Steps 2-6 across the row. You should have 10 stitches; count them to make sure you did not pick up any extra loops along the way.

"Congratulations! You have knit your first row."

To begin the next row, hold the empty needle in your right hand and the needle with the stitches in your left hand. The working yarn hangs straight down from the stitch closest to the tip of the needle **(Photo K)**. Repeat Steps 2-6 across the row.

"Knit a few more rows, have a cup of coffee, and admire what you have knit."

After knitting a few more rows, look closely at your knitting. You will see that each stitch looks like the outlined stitch in **Fig. 3**. You should still have 10 stitches on your needle. If you do, fine; however, if you don't, you probably dropped a stitch or didn't slip off an old stitch. At this point, it is **not** a problem; you are learning something new, and sometimes it takes a little time to do it all correctly. Don't be upset if your work doesn't look very even. This will come with time and practice.

GARTER STITCH

*"Knitting each row, as you have just done, is called Garter Stitch **(Photo L)** and it makes a great scarf. Every two rows form one ridge and it looks the same on both sides. It never rolls and it always lays nice and neat and tidy. If you want to practice your knitting and you really need a scarf, cast on 24 stitches and knit until it is as long as you would like your scarf to be. Turn to the instructions for binding off **(page 8)** and follow them."*

Photo K

working yarn

yarn end

Fig. 3

Photo L   Garter Stitch

LESSON 3 - PURLING

"Purling is almost the reverse of knitting."

If you still have 10 stitches on your needle, use them for Lesson 3. If not, cast on 10 stitches before beginning *(see Lesson 1 - Casting On, pages 2 and 3)*.

ENGLISH METHOD

Step 1: Hold the needle with the stitches in your left hand and the empty needle in your right hand.

Step 2: With the yarn in **front** of the needles, insert the right needle into the front of the stitch from **right** to **left** *(Photo M)*.

Photo M

Step 3: Hold the right needle with your left thumb and index finger while you bring the yarn between the needles from **right** to **left** and around the right needle *(Photo N)*.

Photo N

Step 4: Move the right needle, with the loop of yarn, through the stitch and away from you *(Photo O)*, slipping the old stitch off the left needle. Tighten this new stitch on the shaft of the right needle.

Photo O

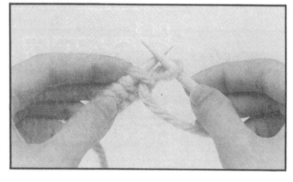

CONTINENTAL METHOD

Step 1: Hold the needle with the stitches in your left hand and the empty needle in your right hand.

Step 2: With the yarn in **front** of the needles, insert the right needle into the front of the stitch from **right** to **left** *(Photo P)*.

Photo P

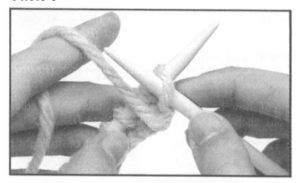

Step 3: With your index finger, bring the yarn between the needles from **right** to **left** and around the right needle *(Photo Q)*.

Photo Q

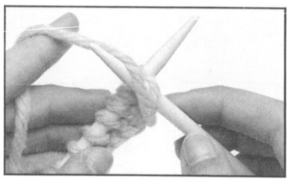

Step 4: Move the right needle, with the loop of yarn, through the stitch and away from you *(Photo R)*, slipping the old stitch off the left needle. Tighten this new stitch on the shaft of the right needle.

Photo R

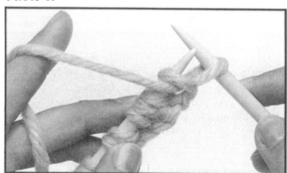

BOTH METHODS

Repeat Steps 2-4 across the row. Make sure you still have 10 stitches.

*"Now do some more rows. This is Garter Stitch, too. Isn't that amazing! The combination of knitting and purling is the foundation of **all** knitting and it enables you to do wonderful things."*

LESSON 4 - STOCKINETTE STITCH

"Now we are going to learn to put knitting and purling together."

Row 1: Knit each stitch across the row *(see Lesson 2, page 4)*.

Row 2: Purl each stitch across the row *(see Lesson 3, page 5)*.

Continue alternating one row of knit and one row of purl, three more times (8 rows).

Notice that the knit side is smooth *(Photo S)* and the purl side is bumpy *(Photo T)*. The knit side is called **Stockinette Stitch** and the purl side is called **Reverse Stockinette Stitch**.

Photo S

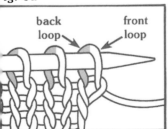

Photo T

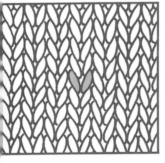

"Refill your coffee cup and admire what you have done."

Look at your work closely. Each knit stitch should look like the outlined stitch in **Fig. 4a**, and each purl stitch should look like the outlined stitch in **Fig. 4b**.

Fig. 4a

Fig. 4b

"When the smooth side is toward you (facing), knit across. When the bumpy side is facing, purl across. You don't have to remember which stitch you did last because you are learning to read your knitting."

Always insert the needle into the **front** loop of the stitch *(Fig. 5a)* to prevent twisting the stitches *(Fig. 5b)*.

Fig. 5a

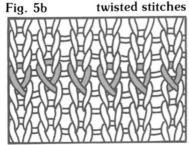

back loop   front loop

Fig. 5b   **twisted stitches**

LESSON 5 - RIBBING

"Ribbing is that wonderful elastic stitch that often appears at the bottom of sweaters, on cuffs and around necklines. It can be done in several combinations of knitting and purling. The most frequently used is knit one stitch, purl one stitch. Until you have mastered the technique, it is easier to work with an even number of stitches."

KNIT 1, PURL 1 RIBBING (abbreviated K1, P1)

Note: Make sure you have an even number of stitches.

Step 1: Knit the first stitch.

Step 2: Bring the yarn **between** the needles from **back** to **front** (ready to purl) *(Fig. 6a)*, and purl the next stitch.

Fig. 6a

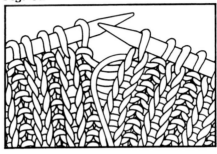

Step 3: Take the yarn **between** the needles to the **back** (ready to knit) *(Fig. 6b)*, and knit the next stitch.

Fig. 6b

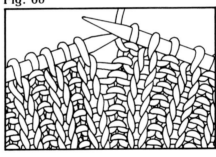

Repeat Steps 2 and 3 across the row.

Now do several more rows. (Begin each new row at Step 1.) Your ribbing should look like **Photo U**.

Photo U

Be sure to move the yarn before each stitch - to the **back** to knit and to the **front** to purl (yarn goes **between** the needles, **not** over it).

*"If you do put the yarn over the needle instead of **between** the needles, you will have an extra stitch and a hole in your work. This is called a 'yarn over' and we're not going to teach you how to do that until page 13."*

Continued on page 7.

RECOGNIZING KNIT AND PURL STITCHES

"Unless you have locked yourself in the bathroom to do your ribbing, it's possible that you've been interrupted in mid-row. That's why it's very important to know the difference in the appearance of the knit and purl stitches."

Once the sequence of stitches is established, you must knit the knit stitches and purl the purl stitches, as they appear on the row being worked in order to have ribbing.

When you pick up your work in mid-row, the needle with the yarn attached always goes in your right hand.

Now look very closely at the stitches just under your left needle. Some of them are V's and some of them are horizontal bars *(Fig. 7)*.

"The V's are saying 'KNIT ME!' and the bars are saying 'PURL ME!'. Try it. It works!"

Fig. 7

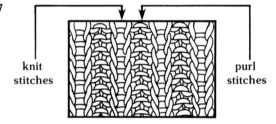

knit stitches   purl stitches

KNIT 2, PURL 2 RIBBING (abbreviated K2, P2)

This is exactly what it says:
Knit 2 stitches, bring yarn forward, purl 2 stitches, take yarn to the back; repeat across the row.
Now do several more rows *(Photo V)*.

Photo V

"Many other combinations of knit and purl stitches can be used to form ribbing. Just remember to knit the knits and purl the purls."

TWISTED RIB

"Sometimes you do twist your stitches on purpose to form a pattern stitch called Twisted Rib."

Twisted Rib is worked just like K1, P1 Ribbing except that each knit stitch is twisted by knitting into the **back** of the stitch *(Fig. 8)* instead of in the usual way.

Fig. 8

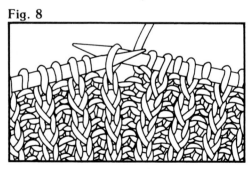

LESSON 6 - DROPPED STITCHES

"If a stitch accidentally drops from your needle, dangles impatiently, gives up and becomes a run - as in a nylon stocking, it is called a 'dropped stitch'.
Knitting would be so much simpler if you could throw all of your dropped stitches into a big box and then, when you dropped another one, you could pick one from the box to replace it.
It won't work. I know, because I've been carrying this box around for years."

There is a better way:
With the knit side facing, insert a crochet hook through the loop of the dropped stitch, hook the strand of yarn immediately above it *(Fig. 9a)*, and pull it through the loop on your hook.

Fig. 9a

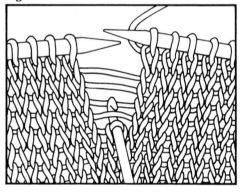

Continue in this manner until you have used all of the strands of yarn. Slip the stitch onto the left hand needle with the right hand side of the stitch to the **front** *(Fig. 9b)*.

Fig. 9b

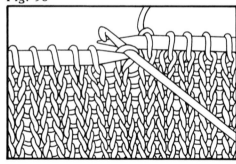

If you drop a purl stitch, **turn** your work around and do the same thing, slipping the stitch onto the **right** hand needle with the right hand side of the stitch to the front. Turn your work again, and continue as before.

"Isn't that incredible? It makes dropping stitches almost fun - but not quite."

7

LESSON 7 - BINDING OFF

*"This **is** fun - besides you have to get those stitches off your needle somehow!"*

All knitting ends with binding off, locking each stitch as you remove it from the needle. Binding off is also used to work buttonholes and pockets and for shaping.

Step 1: Knit 2 stitches.

Step 2: With the **left** needle, bring the first stitch over the second stitch and off the needle **(Figs. 10a & b)**.

Fig. 10a

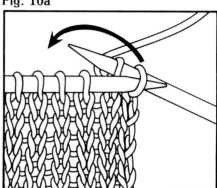

Fig. 10b

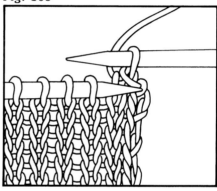

*"You did it! You bound off one stitch. Now let's do it again, but this time you only need to knit **one** stitch because you already have one on your right needle."*

Step 3: Knit the next stitch.
Repeat Steps 2 and 3 until only one stitch remains on the right needle.

Step 4: To lock the last stitch, cut the yarn (leaving a long end) and bring it through the stitch **(Fig. 10c)**, pulling to tighten.

Fig. 10c

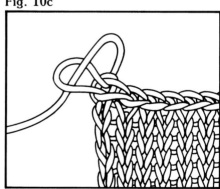

It's **very** important for the bind off to be as elastic as your knitting **(see Binding Off Tips, page 31)**.

"Now it's time to make something real. Let's start with a Slipper because it's quick and easy."

SLIPPER

Cast on 39 stitches.
Row 1: Knit 14 stitches, bring the yarn **between** the needles from **back** to **front**, purl 1 stitch, take the yarn between the needles to the **back**, knit 9 stitches, bring the yarn between the needles to the **front**, purl 1 stitch, take the yarn between the needles to the **back**, knit 14 stitches.
Row 2: Knit each stitch across.
Row 3: Knit 14 stitches, purl 1 stitch, knit 9 stitches, purl 1 stitch, knit 14 stitches. (This is the same as Row 1.)
Row 4: Knit each stitch across.
Rows 5-36: Repeat Rows 3 and 4, 16 times.
Note: You will have 18 ridges on **each** side.

TOE
Row 1: Bind off 5 stitches, knit 8 stitches, purl 1 stitch, knit 9 stitches, purl 1 stitch, knit 14 stitches: you have 34 stitches.
Row 2: Bind off 5 stitches, knit each stitch across: 29 stitches.
Row 3: Work in K1, P1 ribbing across to last stitch, knit 1.
Row 4: Purl 1, work in K1, P1 ribbing across.
Rows 5-14: Repeat Rows 3 and 4, 5 times.

FINISHING
Step 1: Cut the yarn leaving an 18" end. Thread a yarn needle with the end and separately slip each stitch from the knitting needle onto the yarn.
Step 2: Fold the slipper in half lengthwise with **right** sides together (the **right** side is the side with the two long lines of stockinette stitches separating the rows of garter stitch ridges).
Step 3: Pull the yarn **very** tightly gathering all the stitches firmly together and catch the first and last stitches together to secure; do **not** cut yarn.
Step 4: Sew the instep from the toe to the top of the bound off stitches, catching one stitch from each side and being careful to match rows.
Step 5: Weave yarn under several stitches of the seam and cut close to work.
Step 6: Thread a yarn needle with a 16" piece of yarn. Sew the Back seam from the top to the Stockinette Stitch lines and secure. Weave the yarn through each of the remaining 9 stitches; pull **very** tightly and secure.
Step 7: Weave all yarn ends under several stitches and cut close to work.

"Congratulations!
You did it; you made a Slipper.
It doesn't make any difference if this Slipper fits your son, yourself, or your next-door neighbor. The important thing is that you did it - you made it yourself - and you can be very proud of it.
Take a break. Admire what you have done, then go on to learn even more. You are on your way to becoming a full-fledged knitter."

LESSON 8 - SLIP STITCH

When the instructions state slip a stitch, you simply transfer it from one needle to another - generally, from the left needle to the right needle, without knitting or purling it.

In order to prevent twisted stitches, there are times when you should "slip as if to **knit**" - and other times when you should "slip as if to **purl**".

SLIP AS IF TO KNIT

When working a decrease that requires a slipped stitch, insert the right needle into the stitch on the left needle as if you were going to **knit** it *(Fig. 11a)*, and slip it off the left needle.

Fig. 11a

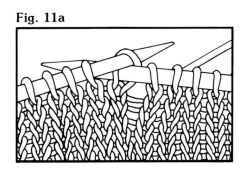

SLIP AS IF TO PURL

When you are working a pattern stitch that requires a slipped stitch that is not part of a decrease, insert the right needle into the stitch on the left needle as if you were going to **purl** it *(Fig. 11b)*, and slip it off the left needle.

Fig. 11b

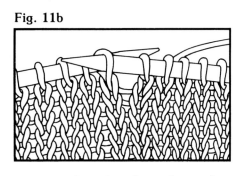

There are two ways a slipped stitch can be used in a pattern when slipped as if to purl.

1. Slip a stitch with the working yarn held on the **wrong** side of the work, so that the working yarn will **not** show *(Fig. 12a)*.

2. Slip a stitch with the working yarn held on the **right** side of the work, so that the working yarn **will** show *(Fig. 12b)*.

Fig. 12a   **Fig. 12b**

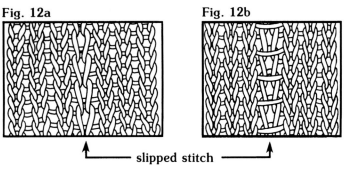

◄——— slipped stitch ———►

To remember which way to slip a stitch, follow this general rule: when you are going to do something with the slipped stitch, as in a decrease, "slip it as if to **knit**"; if not, "slip it as if to **purl**". This will prevent twisted stitches.

LESSON 9 - DECREASING

Some decreases are worked on the knit side and some are worked on the purl side. Some decreases lean to the right and some lean to the left. Decreases worked at the edge of a piece should lean in the SAME direction as the knitting is shaped. They should slant to the **left** on the right side of the garment (#2 or #3) and they should slant to the **right** on the left side (#1). When working decreases that will be visible, it is the direction of the slant, as it appears on the right side of the work, that is important.

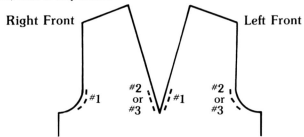

KNIT DECREASES

Work a few rows in Stockinette Stitch between each decrease, ending by working a purl row.

1. KNIT 2 STITCHES TOGETHER (abbreviated K2 tog)
Insert the right needle into the **front** of the first two stitches on the left needle as if to **knit** *(Fig. 13)* and knit them together as if they were one stitch. This decrease slants to the right *(Photo W)* and is one of the most frequently used.

Fig. 13   **Photo W**

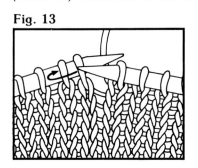

Work a few rows in Stockinette Stitch between each decrease, ending by working a purl row.

2. SLIP 1, KNIT 1, PASS THE SLIPPED STITCH OVER (abbreviated slip 1, K1, PSSO)
Slip one stitch as if to **knit**. Knit the next stitch. With the left needle, bring the slipped stitch over the knit stitch *(Fig. 14)* and off the needle, just as you did when you were binding off. This decrease slants to the left *(Photo X)*.

Fig. 14   **Photo X**

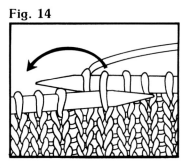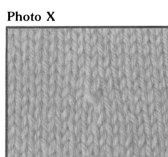

3. SLIP, SLIP, KNIT (abbreviated SSK)

Slip the first stitch as if to **knit** *(Fig. 15a)*, then slip the next stitch as if to **knit**. Insert the **left** needle into the **front** of both slipped stitches *(Fig. 15b)* and knit them together *(Fig. 15c)*. This decrease also slants to the left *(Photo Y)* and is interchangeable with slip 1, K1, PSSO. However, because SSK is closest to K2 tog in appearance, it is often used when the decreases will be visible, as in Raglan Sleeve Sweaters.

Fig. 15a

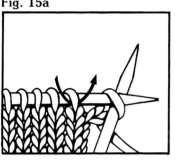

Fig. 15b

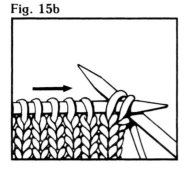

Fig. 15c

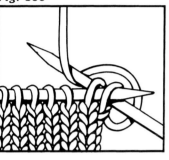

Photo Y

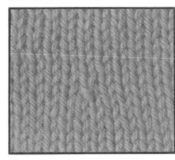

PURL DECREASES

Generally, knitting instructions are written so the decreases are worked on the knit side. However, sometimes it is necessary to work them on the purl side.

Continue to work a few rows in Stockinette Stitch between each decrease, ending by working a **knit** row.

1. PURL 2 STITCHES TOGETHER (abbreviated P2 tog)

Insert the right needle into the **front** of the first two stitches on the left needle as if to **purl** *(Fig. 16)* and purl them together. This decrease slants to the right on the knit side of the work *(Photo Z)* and is the most common purl decrease.

Fig. 16

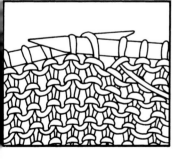

Photo Z

2. SLIP, SLIP, PURL (abbreviated SSP)

Slip the first stitch as if to **knit**, then slip the next stitch as if to **knit**. Place these two stitches back onto the left needle. Insert the right needle into the **back** of both stitches from **back** to **front** *(Fig. 17)* and purl them together. This decrease slants to the left on the knit side *(Photo AA)* and resembles SSK.

Fig. 17

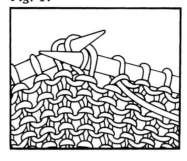

Photo AA

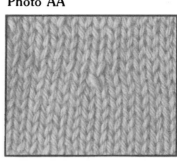

TWISTED STITCH DECREASES

Occasionally, a pattern stitch may call for intentionally twisted stitches as part of the design. This is the only time the following decreases should be used.

1. KNIT 2 STITCHES TOGETHER THROUGH THE BACK LOOPS (abbreviated K2 tog TBL)

Insert the right needle into the **back** of the first two stitches on the left needle from **front** to **back** *(Fig. 18)* and knit them together. This decrease slants to the left *(Photo BB)*.

Fig. 18

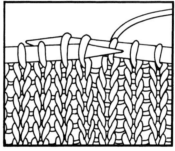

Photo BB

2. PURL 2 STITCHES TOGETHER THROUGH THE BACK LOOPS (abbreviated P2 tog TBL)

Insert the right needle into the **back** of both stitches from **back** to **front** *(Fig. 19)* and purl them together. This decrease also slants to the left on the knit side *(Photo CC)*.

Fig. 19

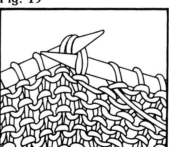

Photo CC

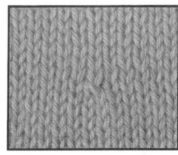

LESSON 10 - INCREASING

"If you are worried that all of those stitches you just decreased can never be replaced, you can relax - it's time to learn how to add stitches and shape your knitting."

Continue to work a few rows in Stockinette Stitch between each increase.

KNIT INCREASES

1. BAR INCREASE
Knit the next stitch but do **not** slip it off the left needle **(Fig. 20a)**. Instead, knit into the **back** of the **same** stitch **(Fig. 20b)** and slip it off the left needle.

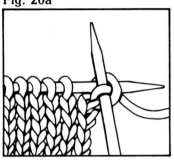

Fig. 20a

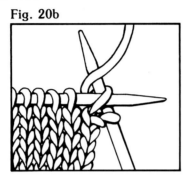

Fig. 20b

*"You are now the proud owner of a brand new stitch that sits on top of a small bar **(Photo below)**. You have created two stitches from one stitch."*

The Bar Increase is the most popular and, perhaps, the easiest of increases. It is often used at the beginning and at the end of a row where it probably would be hidden in a seam.

2. YARN OVER INCREASE (abbreviated YO)
A Yarn Over is simply placing the yarn over the right needle creating an extra stitch **(Figs. 30a-d, page 13)**. Since the Yarn Over Increase does produce a hole in the knit fabric, it is used for a lacy effect **(Photo below)**.

"If you are going to use this increase, be sure that you want a nice, round, chubby hole."

On the row following a Yarn Over, you must be careful to keep it on the needle and treat it as a stitch by knitting or purling it as instructed.

3. MAKE ONE (abbreviated M1)
Insert the **left** needle under the horizontal strand between the stitches from the **front (Fig. 21a)**. Then, knit into the **back** of the strand **(Fig. 21b)**.

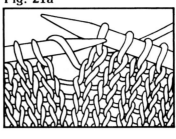

Fig. 21a

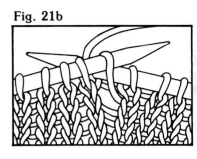

Fig. 21b

*"Your new stitch is intentionally twisted in order to prevent a hole, but it is 'almost' invisible **(Photo below)**."*

The Make One is used when working increases that will not be hidden in a seam, and is most commonly used when knitting from the neck down.

4. INVISIBLE INCREASES
Right Invisible Increase
Insert the right needle from the **front** into the side of the stitch **below** the next stitch on the left needle **(Fig. 22)** and knit it.

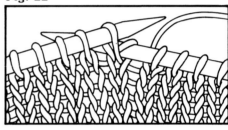

Fig. 22

Left Invisible Increase
Insert the **left** needle from the **back** into the side of the stitch 2 rows **below** the stitch on the right needle **(Fig. 23a)**, pull it up and knit into the **back** loop **(Fig. 23b)**.

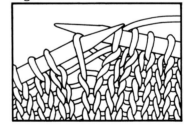

Fig. 23a

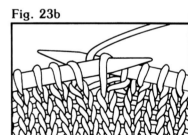

Fig. 23b

Caution: Invisible Increases **(Photos below)** cause some "pulling" of the knit fabric and should not be used for raglan shaping or when knitting from the neck down.

Bar Increase	Yarn Over Increase	Make One	Right Invisible Increase	Left Invisible Increase

PURL INCREASES

"Sometimes, it will be necessary to make a purl increase - it's not quite as much fun as making a knit increase, but of course you can do it. You're very talented."

1. BAR INCREASE

Purl the next stitch but do **not** slip it off the left needle. Insert the right needle into the **back** loop of the **same** stitch from **back** to **front** (*Fig. 24*) and purl it. Slip it off the needle.

Fig. 24

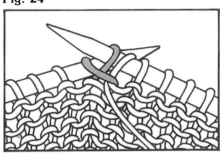

2. MAKE ONE PURL (abbreviated M1P)

Insert the **left** needle under the horizontal strand between the stitches from the **front** (*Fig. 25a*). Then, purl into the **back** of the strand (*Fig. 25b*).

Fig. 25a

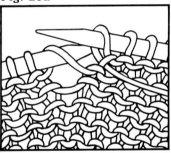

Fig. 25b

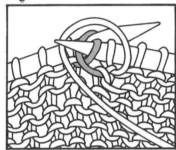

3. INVISIBLE INCREASES

Right Invisible Increase

Insert the right needle from the **back** into the top of the stitch **below** the next stitch on the left needle (*Fig. 26*) and purl it.

Left Invisible Increase

Insert the **left** needle from the **front** into the top of the stitch 2 rows **below** the stitch on the right needle (*Fig. 27*), pull it up and purl it.

Fig. 26

Fig. 27

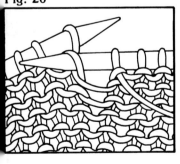
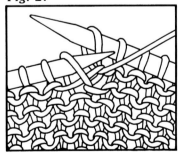

COMBINATION INCREASES

1. KNITTING AND PURLING INTO THE SAME STITCH

Knit the next stitch but do **not** slip it off the left needle. Bring the yarn to the **front** (between the needles) and purl into the **front** loop of the **same** stitch (*Fig. 28*). Slip it off the needle.

Fig. 28

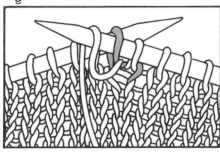

2. PURLING AND KNITTING INTO THE SAME STITCH

Purl the next stitch but do **not** slip it off the left needle. Bring the yarn to the **back** (between the needles) and knit into the **back** loop of the **same** stitch (*Fig. 29*). Slip it off the needle.

Fig. 29

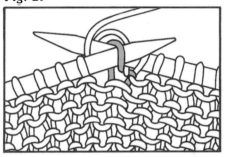

LESSON 11 - YARN OVERS

1. When a Yarn Over (abbreviated YO) falls **between 2 knit stitches**, work as follows:
Bring the yarn forward **between** the needles, then back **over** the top of the right needle, so that it is now in position to knit the next stitch **(Fig. 30a)**.

Fig. 30a

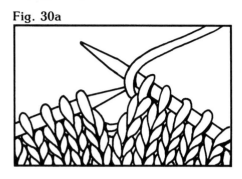

2. When a YO falls **after a knit stitch and before a purl stitch**, work as follows:
Bring the yarn forward **between** the needles, then back **over** the top of the right needle and forward **between** the needles again, so that it is now in position to purl the next stitch **(Fig. 30b)**.

Fig. 30b

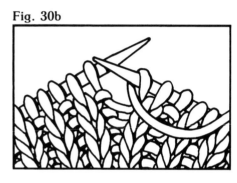

3. When a YO falls **between 2 purl stitches**, work as follows:
Take the yarn **over** the right needle to the back, then forward **under** it, so that it is now in position to purl the next stitch **(Fig. 30c)**.

Fig. 30c

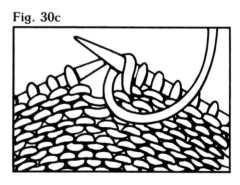

4. When a YO falls **after a purl stitch and before a knit stitch**, work as follows:
Take the yarn **over** the right needle to the back, so that it is now in position to knit the next stitch **(Fig. 30d)**.

Fig. 30d

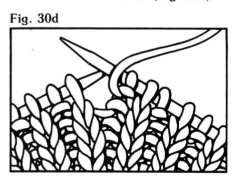

"Besides being used to increase, Yarn Overs can be used to create lace patterns. These patterns are guaranteed to impress your friends, family, neighbors, and any strangers who might be passing by!"

When working a lace pattern, a YO will be preceded by or followed by a decrease, so that the total number of stitches remains the same.

Work a few rows in Stockinette Stitch on an even number of stitches, ending by working a purl row.
Now, work the Eyelet Row across:

K1, ★ YO, K2 tog; repeat from ★ across to last st, K1.

Note: A star (★) tells you where to begin a repeat **(see Terms, page 15)**.

Work some more rows in Stockinette Stitch so that the Eyelet Row will be centered in your swatch.
(Note that the total number of stitches remains the same.)

*"See the holes in the fabric.
This is your Eyelet Row and you have just followed a simple Lace Pattern.
This can be used alone, or with a ribbon woven through it for a decorative or useful touch, or you can fold the swatch along the Eyelet Row to form a picot edging **(Photo DD)**."*

Photo DD

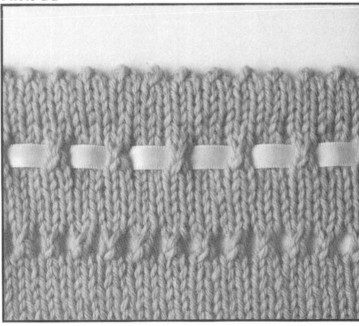

LESSON 12 - GAUGE

TRUST ME; IT'S IMPORTANT!

"Gauge and accurate body measurements are the two most important ingredients in guaranteeing that your garment will fit. This is carved in stone."

Gauge is the number of stitches and rows in every inch of your knitting and is used to control the finished size. All knitting patterns specify the gauge, or tension, that the designer used - **and that you must match to insure proper size.**

Because everyone knits differently - loosely, tightly, or somewhere in between - the finished size can vary even when the knitters use the very same pattern, yarn, and needles.

Before beginning any knit item, it is **absolutely** necessary for you to knit a swatch, in the pattern stitch with the yarn and needles suggested. It must be large enough for you to measure your gauge, usually 4" x 4".

YARN: Worsted Weight
NEEDLES: Size 7 (4.50 mm)
GAUGE: In Stockinette Stitch, 20 sts and 26 rows = 4"

Cast on 20 stitches.
Work in Stockinette Stitch for 26 rows and then bind off. Lay your swatch **wrong** side up on a hard, smooth, flat surface. Then measure it to see if it measures 4" x 4" **(Photo EE)**. If it is smaller than 4", you are knitting too tightly - try again with larger size needles. If it is larger than 4", you are knitting too loosely - try again with smaller size needles.
A slight variation in gauge will be multiplied and much more evident over a greater number of stitches. For instance, if you are knitting a sweater with a finished measurement of 34", and your gauge is 5½ stitches per inch instead of 5, the finished sweater will measure only 31", a difference of 3". If knitting an afghan, the difference would be even more dramatic.
Keep trying until **your** swatch measures 4" x 4".

"Congratulations! Now you are ready to start knitting whatever it was that you really wanted to make when I made you stop and knit a 4 inch square."

Making an accurate gauge swatch, **each** time you begin something new, does take time. But, spending weeks or months working on an item that ends up several sizes too small or too large is frustrating, unnecessary, and a waste of time.

"It's really important for you to realize that this swatch does not guarantee that your gauge will not change as you knit. Many things can affect your tension. A glass of wine could result in a larger piece of knitting, and an exciting football game can leave your palms damp, and your knitting smaller than you expected.
To guard against these nightmares, measure the total width of your piece every 3 or 4 inches, and remember you can correct these problems by changing needle size. It won't show (I promise) and it will put you back on gauge. It's also possible that you may have to rip back a bit. If so, be brave. Great knitters are good rippers."

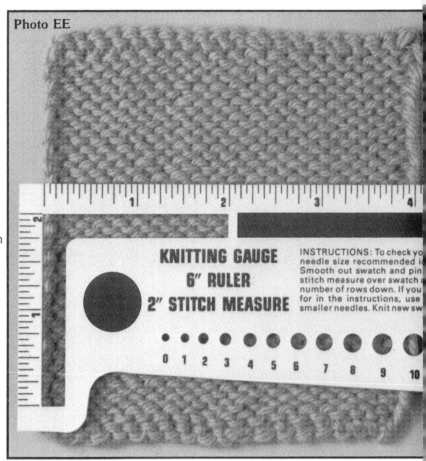

Photo EE

KNITTING GAUGE
6" RULER
2" STITCH MEASURE

INSTRUCTIONS: To check yo needle size recommended i Smooth out swatch and pin stitch measure over swatch number of rows down. If you for in the instructions, use smaller needles. Knit new sw

0 1 2 3 4 5 6 7 8 9 10

LESSON 13 - RIPPING BACK

"If you cannot correct a mistake by dropping a stitch and picking it back up, then the only thing to do is to take a deep breath and two aspirin and start ripping."

If the mistake is **on the row you just worked**, turn the work around so that you are holding the needle with the mistake on it in your left hand. ★ Insert the **right** needle from the **back** into the stitch **below** the next stitch on the left needle **(Fig. 31)**, slip the stitch off the **left** needle and gently pull the working yarn to unravel the old stitch; repeat from ★ across until the mistake has been eliminated. Turn your work again and continue as before.

Fig. 31

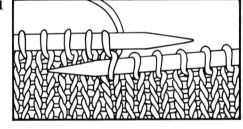

If you discover a mistake **in a previous row** or if you have not maintained correct gauge, it will be necessary to rip out more than one row.
Place a safety pin or paper clip through the first **and** last stitch in the row with the mistake.
Slide all the stitches off the needles and rip back to the first safety pin or paper clip. Hold your knitting in your left hand with the working yarn at the right. ★ Insert a needle, from the **back**, into the stitch **below** the first stitch and gently pull the working yarn to unravel the old stitch. Repeat from ★ until all the stitches are back on a needle. ***Note:*** There will be much less chance of dropping or splitting stitches if the stitches are picked up with a needle 2 or 3 sizes smaller.

LESSON 14 - HOW TO READ INSTRUCTIONS

Knitting instructions often seem to be written in another language because of the many abbreviations and unfamiliar terms. However, instructions are actually easier to follow once you understand this knitting shorthand.
Generally a list of abbreviations is included with a pattern. Those most frequently used by *Leisure Arts* are listed below:

ABBREVIATIONS

approx	approximately
BC	Back Cable or Back Cross
beg	beginning
BO	bind off
CB	Cable Back
CC	Contrasting Color
CF	Cable Front
ch	chain
CO	cast on
dec	decrease
dp	double point
EOR	every other row
est	established
FC	Front Cable or Front Cross
fig	figure
gms or gr	gram(s)
inc	increase
K	knit
LT	Left Twist
M1	Make One
M1P	Make One Purl
MC	Main Color
mm	millimeters
oz	ounce(s)
P	purl
patt	pattern
pg(s)	page(s)
prev	previous
PSSO	pass slipped stitch over
rem	remain(s)(ing)
rep	repeat
rib	ribbing
Rnd(s)	Round(s)
RT	Right Twist
sc	single crochet
sk	skip
sl	slip
sp(s)	space(s)
SSK	slip, slip, knit
st(s)	stitch(es)
St St or Stock St	Stockinette Stitch
TB	Twist Back
tbl	through back loop(s)
TF	Twist Front
tog	together
TR	Twisted Rib
wt	weight
WYB or WYIB	with yarn in back
WYF or WYIF	with yarn in front
YO	yarn over
§	marker (place or slip)

TERMS

★ — work instructions following ★ (star) as many **more** times as indicated in addition to the first time.

† to † — work all instructions from first † (dagger) to second † **as many** times as specified.

AT THE SAME TIME — two different shapings are worked simultaneously, while maintaining the established pattern.

change to larger size needles — replace the right needle with the larger needle and work the stitches from the left needle as instructed; replace the left needle with the other larger size needle.

change to smaller size needles — replace the right needle with the smaller needle and work the stitches from the left needle as instructed; replace the left needle with the other smaller size needle.

loosely — (binding off or casting on) the work should be as elastic as the knitting.

marker — a small piece of yarn tied in a circle, a rubber band, or a small plastic ring.

multiple — the number of stitches required to complete one repeat of a pattern.

place marker — slip a marker on the needle to mark or set off a group of stitches or to mark the beginning of a round. Slip it from the left needle to the right needle on every row (or round) until you are instructed to remove it or until it is no longer needed.

right vs left — the side of the garment as if you were wearing it.

right side vs wrong side — the right side of your work is the side the 'neighbors' will see.

work even — work without increasing or decreasing in the established pattern.

work across — continue working in the established pattern.

PUNCTUATION

When reading knitting instructions, read from punctuation mark to punctuation mark. Just as in grammar, commas (,) mean to pause and semicolons (;) mean to stop.

colon (:) — the number(s) given after a colon at the end of a row or round denote(s) the number of stitches you should have on your needle.

parentheses ( ) or brackets [ ] — work enclosed instructions **as many** times as specified by the number immediately following **or** work all enclosed instructions in the stitch or space indicated **or** contains explanatory remarks.

KNIT TERMINOLOGY	
UNITED STATES	**INTERNATIONAL**
gauge	= tension
bind off	= cast off
yarn over (YO)	= yarn forward (yfwd) **or** yarn around needle (yrn)

KNITTING NEEDLES															
U.S.	0	1	2	3	4	5	6	7	8	9	10	10½	11	13	15	17
English/U.K.	13	12	11	10	9	8	7	6	5	4	3	2	1	00	000	---
Metric - mm	2.00	2.25	2.75	3.25	3.50	3.75	4.00	4.50	5.00	5.50	6.00	6.50	8.00	9.00	10.00	12.75

LESSON 15 - SIZING

HOW TO DECIDE WHICH SIZE TO KNIT

Most garment patterns are written for at least three different sizes. The instructions usually include both the actual bust/chest measurement and the finished measurement of the garment.

To decide which size to knit, first consider whether you want a loose-fitting or a snug-fitting garment. Then measure around the fullest part of the bust/chest and compare this measurement to the sizes given. Be sure to take an accurate measurement. Choose the size based on the actual measurement or on the finished measurement.

At this point, you may want to measure a favorite sweater with similar styling, and knit the size that has the nearest finished measurement.

> "CAUTION: Because you always buy a ready-made size 40, does not necessarily mean that you want to knit a size 40.
>
> ADDITIONAL CAUTION: If you wear a size 34 bra, this is not a guarantee that your bust measurement is 34 inches."

HOW TO MEASURE

Once you have decided which size to knit, you may need to adjust the body length and sleeve length in the instructions according to actual measurements.

To measure body length, place the tape measure approximately 1¾" down from the underarm and let the tape measure hang straight with your arm at your side. Again, you may want to measure that favorite sweater.

When the instructions tell you how many inches to knit the garment before beginning the armhole shaping, you can now adjust this length to your measurement.

Measure the sleeve length in the same way you measured the body length, being sure your arm is straight at your side.

MEASURING CHILDREN

The only accurate way to determine which size to knit for a child is to measure the child. Measure the child's chest approximately 2" below the underarm and choose the size that has the nearest actual measurement. It is also important to measure the arm length and the body length to make any necessary adjustments to the instructions.

> "Do not panic if you find that your 8 year old only needs a size 4 — or that your sturdy 6 year old will really need a size 10. Children come in more shapes and sizes than grown-ups and usually refuse to fit into size or age brackets."

MEASURING YOUR KNITTING

Many instructions include schematics **(below)** of the garment, indicating the finished measurements of each piece, for your reference as you measure your knitting.

Always measure your knitting on a hard, smooth, flat surface, without either scrunching or stretching the piece.

It is important to measure the width of your piece every three or four inches to make sure your gauge remains consistent. The dotted lines on the schematics indicate the beginning of any shaping.

Measure the armholes from the dotted line to the dotted line at the shoulder shaping. Measure the length to the underarm along the line indicated, from the bottom of the cast on edge to the beginning of the armhole shaping and measure the armholes from the dotted line to the dotted line at the neck shaping. The Sleeve length is measured from the bottom of the cast on edge to the begining of the sleeve cap and the sleeve cap is measured from dotted line to dotted line. When measuring a raglan armhole, measure along the line indicated **(Fig. 32)**.

Fig. 32

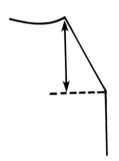

SCHEMATICS

| BACK | FRONT | SLEEVE |

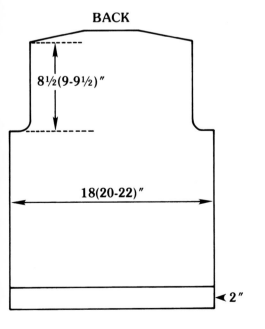

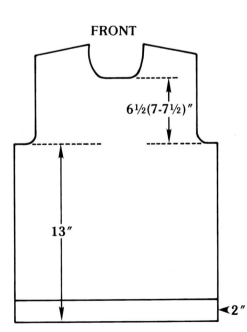

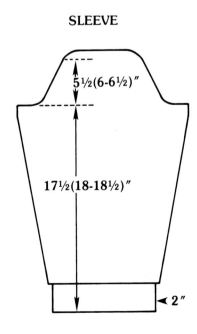

All measurements are approximate.

LESSON 16 - MATERIALS
"Don't stop yet, there is still lots to learn."

YARN

WEIGHTS
Yarn weight (type or size) is divided into four basic categories.

Fingering: Fine weight yarns that make great socks and beautiful baby clothes.
Needles: sizes 1-4
Gauge: 6½ to 7½ sts per inch

Sport: Most often used for light-weight sweaters and baby afghans.
Needles: sizes 4-6
Gauge: 5½ to 6 sts per inch

Worsted: Makes great sweaters, vests, and afghans.
Needles: sizes 7 or 8
Gauge: 4½ to 5 sts per inch

Bulky: Generally used to make heavy sweaters, jackets, and coats.
Needles: sizes 9-17
Gauge: 2 to 4 sts per inch

Note: Baby yarn falls into two categories - Fingering or Sport. Check the yarn label for the recommended gauge.

These weights have absolutely nothing to do with ply. Ply refers to the number of strands that have been twisted together to make the yarn. There are fingering weight yarns consisting of four plies - and there are bulky weight yarns made of a single ply.

FIBERS
There are many, many, many of these.

Wool: Warm, naturally elastic, holds its shape well and usually should be hand washed or dry cleaned.

Man-Made Fibers: Generally less expensive, machine washable and dryable.

Cotton: Cool, little elasticity, hand wash.

Silk: Strong, little elasticity, dry clean.

Blends: You name it, they've made it.

SUBSTITUTING YARN
Once you know the **weight** of the yarn specified for a particular pattern, **any** brand of the **same** weight may be used for that pattern.
You may wish to purchase a single skein first, and knit a gauge swatch. Compare the gauge (remember, it **must** match) and then compare the way the new yarn looks to the photograph to be sure that you'll be satisfied with the results. How many skeins to buy depends on the yardage. Compare the labels and don't hesitate to ask the shopowner for assistance. Ounces and grams can vary from one brand of the same weight to another, but the yardage required to make a garment, in the size and pattern you've chosen, will always remain the same.

DYE LOTS
Yarn is dyed in "lots" and then numbered. Different lots of the same color will vary slightly in shade and will be noticeable if knit in the same piece.
When buying yarn, it is important to check labels for the dye lot number. You should purchase enough of one color, from the same lot, to finish the entire project. It is a good practice to purchase an extra skein to be sure that you have enough to complete your project.

CARE AND MAINTENANCE SYMBOLS
Yarn manufacturers have established a set of universal symbols to help you care for your completed work. You should become familiar with these symbols.

FIVE BASIC SYMBOLS

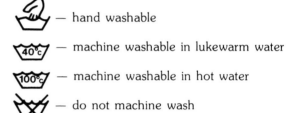

— **wash tub:** laundering or washing instructions

— **triangle:** bleaching instructions

— **square:** machine drying instructions

— **hand iron:** pressing or ironing instructions

— **circle or dry-cleaning cylinder:** dry-cleaning instructions

ADDITIONAL INFORMATION

Washing Instructions

— hand washable

— machine washable in lukewarm water

— machine washable in hot water

— do not machine wash

Bleaching Instructions

— use chlorine bleach as directed on container label

— do not use chlorine bleach

Drying Instructions

— may be dried in a tumble dryer

— should be dried on a flat surface

Ironing Instructions

— hot iron, if required

— warm iron, if required

— cool iron, if required

— do not iron

Dry-cleaning Instructions

— dry-cleanable, any solvent may be used

— dry-cleanable, any solvent may be used except trichlorethylene

— dry-cleanable, using petroleum or fluorocarbon solvents only

— do not dry-clean

NEEDLES

"This seems to be a law of nature: whatever pattern you fall madly in love with, will usually call for needles that you don't have. Think of each purchase as an investment in the future."

SIZES

The size of a needle refers to the diameter of the shaft and is measured in millimeters. Most instructions give a recommended needle size, followed by the equivalent millimeter size. American and English needles are labeled differently, so it is best to purchase new needles according to millimeters. The chart below lists American needle sizes with their English and metric (mm) equivalents.

TYPES

Aluminum: Aluminum needles do not bend or break. Their smooth surface rarely develops fiber-catching burrs, and they make a very professional clicking sound as you knit. Many aluminum needles are treated with protective finishes to insure durability. The smaller sizes are very practical, but some knitters have found the larger sizes to be too heavy.

Plastic: Plastic needles are lightweight, less slippery than aluminum, and make less noise when knitting. They will bend, but tend to break when exposed to extreme temperatures.

Bamboo: Bamboo needles have a polished, smooth surface, are lightweight, and tap quietly as you knit. Extra care is required to prevent scratches on the shaft of these needles because they might snag the yarn.

Wood: Wood needles are difficult to obtain and are less likely to be accurately sized. Wood needles may develop fiber-catching burrs.

SHAPES

Single Point: Single point needles come in 10 and 14 inch lengths and have a knob at one end. Knobs may be round or flat (to prevent rolling). The needle size is usually printed on the knob. They generally hold four times their length in gathered fabric.

Double Point: Double point needles come in sets of four and in various lengths from 7 to 12 inches. They are used for small tubular pieces such as mittens and hats.

Circular: Circular needles are the most versatile of all knitting needles and are available in 11 to 39 inch lengths. They consist of two short needles joined by a nylon cable. Circular needles can be used for both round (seamless) and flat knitting. They are ideal when knitting large tubes, such as a skirt or the body of a sweater, or when you have too many stitches for a straight needle. Circular needles distribute the weight of the knitting evenly and place less physical strain on your arms and shoulders.

KNITTING GOODIES

"These are all the things that make your life as a knitter easier and seem to really impress your non-knitting friends. None of them are essential. Many of them will make you wonder how you ever lived without them."
(Photo, pages 19 and 20).

STITCH HOLDERS

They hold your stitches, when you are told to slip them off the needle, until you are ready to knit them later. They are available in different lengths and styles; some feature a coiled spring closure and some resemble large safety pins.

MARKERS

These fit on your needles and you slip them from the left needle to the right needle as you are working. The markers tell you - "You're going to do something different now". They are available in different sizes and colors.

POINT PROTECTORS

These are available in different sizes. They slip on the points of your needles when you put your knitting down. They probably do protect the points; but mostly, they keep your stitches from falling off the ends of the needles.

ROW COUNTERS

These either slip on your needle to be turned after each row or are held independently and a button must be pushed after each row. Both will keep track of the rows that you have knit, but they are **not** automatic.

CABLE NEEDLES

These have a point on each end and you use them when you work a cable. They are available in several shapes and sizes. The size of the cable needle does not have to be the same size as the needles with which you are knitting, but it should not be bigger or it will stretch the stitches out of shape.

GAUGE RULER

This is a multi-talented little gadget. It is placed on your knitting to help you count the number of stitches and rows to check your gauge. In addition, there is a row of carefully gauged circles on one side. You can insert your circular and double pointed needles through these circles to determine their size.

BOBBINS

You wind your assorted colors of yarn on these when you are knitting an argyle pattern, or any pattern where you do not carry the background color along the wrong side of the knitting.

Every good knitting bag would also contain the following: Scissors, pen or pencil and paper, a measuring tape, safety pins, a line keeper for use with charts, yarn threaders, yarn needles, crochet hooks, and blocking pins or T-pins (rustproof).

Of course, the ultimate luxury is to have a knitting bag with lots of pockets or dividers, cases to protect your knitting needles and crochet hooks, and a plastic bag to help keep your knitting clean.

KNITTING NEEDLES - CONVERSION CHART																		
American	0	1	2	3	4	5	6	7	8	9	10	10½	11	13	15	17	19	35
English	13	12	11	10	9	8	7	6	5	4	3	2	1	00	000	—	—	—
Metric - mm	2.00	2.25	2.75	3.25	3.50	3.75	4.25	4.50	5.00	5.50	6.00	6.50	8.00	9.00	10.00	12.00	15.00	20.00

KNITTING GOODIES

KEY:
1. Tape measure
2. Cable needles
3. Stitch holders
4. Row counter
5. Pins
6. Scissors
7. Yarn needle
8. Circular needles
   (No. 7 and No. 17)
9. Double point needles
10. Markers
11. Bobbins
12. Point protector
13. Crochet hook
14. Gauge ruler
15. Straight needles

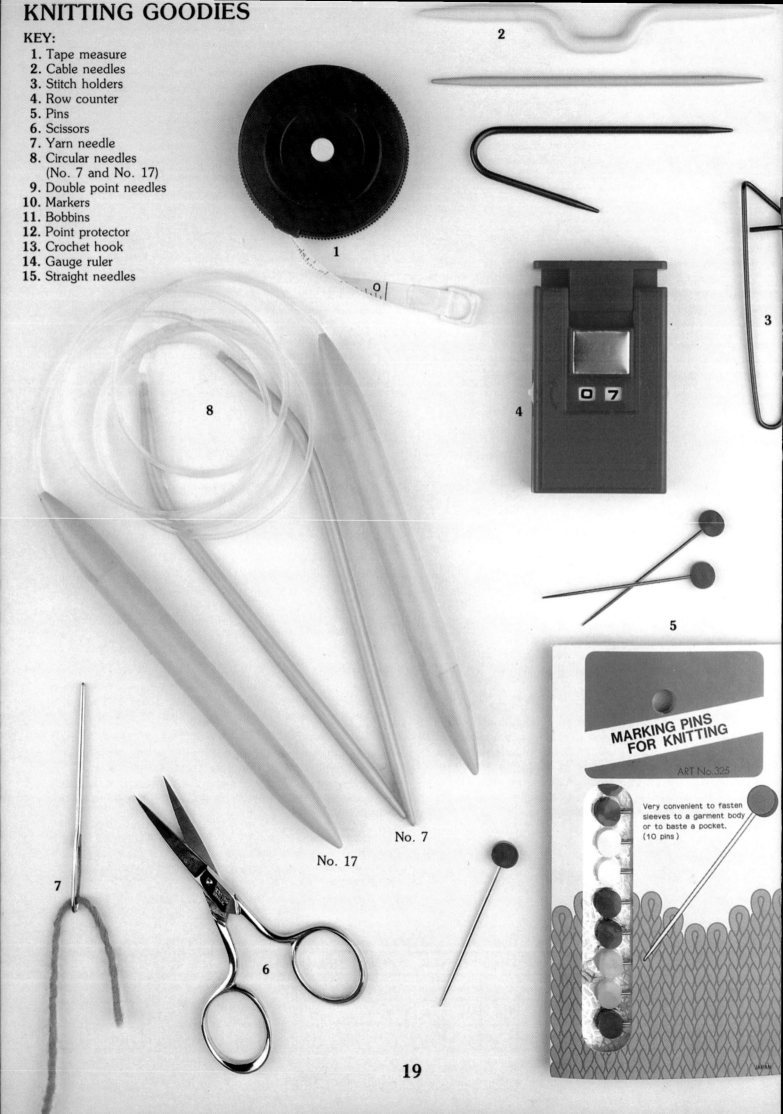

No. 7

No. 17

MARKING PINS FOR KNITTING

ART No.325

Very convenient to fasten sleeves to a garment body or to baste a pocket.
(10 pins)

19

9

3

4

1

10

12

15

No. 0

No. 1

No. 2

No. 3

No. 4

No. 5

No. 6

No. 7

No. 8

No. 9

No. 10

No. 10½

No. 11

No. 13

No. 15

14

KNITTING GAUGE
6" RULER
2" STITCH MEASURE

0 1 2 3 4 5 6 7 8 9 10 10½ 11 13 15

INSTRUCTIONS: To check your gauge, cast on 20 to 30 stitches, using needle size recommended in instructions. Knit 3" in pattern stitch. Smooth out swatch and don't stretch. Place Boye 2" stitch measure over swatch and count number of stitches across and number of rows down. If you have more stitches and rows than called for in the instructions, use larger needles. If you have fewer, use smaller needles. Knit new swatches and re-check until gauge is correct.

11

13

20

LESSON 17 - FINISHING

"I know you've been waiting for this. This is the section that will help you to make your knit garments look 'handmade' instead of 'homemade'."

SEAMS

A tapestry or a yarn needle is best for seams because the blunt point will not split the yarn. Use the yarn the garment was made with, to sew the seams. If the yarn is textured or bulky, it will be easier to sew the seam with a finer, smoother yarn of the same color. Tapestry yarn or an acrylic needlepoint yarn work well. Be sure the care of the yarns is the same - if the yarn used to knit the garment is machine washable, the seam yarn must also be machine washable.
A little advance planning will prevent an unpleasant surprise.

SHOULDER SEAMS
Weaving

Shoulder seams that are joined by weaving appear seamless. With the **right** side of both pieces facing you and the edges even, bring the needle from behind the work and through the center of the first stitch, leaving a long end to be woven in later. ★ Bring the needle over the top of the seam and pick up both loops of the corresponding stitch on the second piece **(Fig. 33a)**. Bring the needle back over the seam and pick up the inverted V of the next stitch **(Fig. 33b)**. Repeat from ★ across, smoothing the "steps" of the bind off as you go. Pull the yarn gently every 2 or 3 stitches, being careful to maintain even tension.

Fig. 33a   **Fig. 33b**

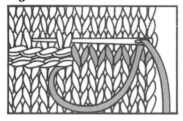   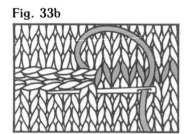

Backstitch

Backstitching provides a firm shoulder seam. The seam should be sewn about one row in from the bound off edges. If the garment has shoulder shaping, the seam should slant slightly from the neck to the shoulder, following the slant of the bound off stitches. The "steps" of the bind off may be used like notches in sewing, to help line up the stitches. With the **right** sides together and edges even, weave the end of the yarn through 5 or 6 of the bound off stitches to secure it. Insert the needle from **front** to **back** at the edge of the seam, then bring it up from **back** to **front** a half stitch forward (at 1) **(Fig. 34a)**. Insert the needle back where the first stitch began (at 2) and bring it up a whole stitch forward (at 3). ★ Insert the needle a half stitch back from the yarn (at 1) **(Fig. 34b)** and up again a whole stitch forward (at 4). Repeat from the ★ across. With each stitch, you are going back a half stitch and then forward a whole stitch. At the end of the seam, weave your yarn back into the seam for 5 or 6 stitches and cut the yarn close to the work.

Fig. 34a   **Fig. 34b**

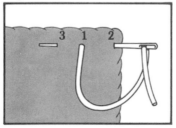

SLEEVE SEAMS

"Sleeves come in various styles. Sometimes they are knit on by picking up stitches along the armhole but, more often they are sewn in".

Sleeves With Caps

When a Sleeve has shaping at the top to match the armhole, the shaping is called the Sleeve Cap.
Fold the Sleeve in half lengthwise to find the center of the cap. With **right** sides together, pin the center of the Cap to the shoulder seam **(Fig. 35)**. Pin the underarm bound off stitches of the body to those of the Sleeve. Pin the Sleeve in place, easing in any fullness. Backstitch this seam, one stitch in from the edge, with the Body side toward you so that you can follow a line of purl stitches.

Fig. 35

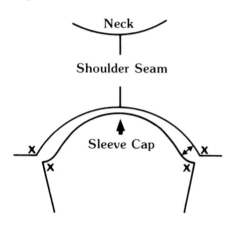

Drop Shoulder Sleeves

Garments without armhole shaping have "dropped shoulders". Fold the Sleeve in half lengthwise to find the center of the bound off edge. With **right** sides together, pin the center of the edge to the shoulder seam **(Fig. 36)**. The instructions or schematics will tell you the length of the armhole. Measure this length down from the shoulder seam in Front and pin one end of the Sleeve; repeat for the Back. Pin the rest of the Sleeve in place, easing in any fullness. Backstitch this seam, one stitch in from the edge, with the Body side toward you so that you can follow a line of purl stitches.

Fig. 36

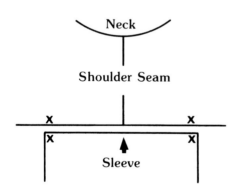

Raglan Sleeves

Raglan shaping begins at the underarm and continues in a gradual slant to the neckline. Usually, there is no shoulder seam.
With **right** sides together, pin the underarm bound off stitches of the Front to those of the Sleeve and Backstitch this small area, one stitch in from the edge. Weave the rest of this seam using Vertical Weaving **(Fig. 37 or Fig. 38, page 22)**. Repeat for the Back seam and for the second Sleeve.

UNDERARM AND SIDE SEAMS

It is usually best to weave the side and underarm seams because weaving is practically invisible.

Vertical Weaving - One Stitch In

With the **right** side of both pieces facing you and edges even, sew through both sides once to secure the beginning of the seam. Pull the first and second stitches on the Front edge slightly apart. Notice the bars between the stitches. Insert the needle under the bar **between** the first and second stitches on the first row and pull the yarn through *(Fig. 37)*. Insert the needle under the next bar on the second side. Repeat from side to side being careful to match rows. Repeat this process about six times on each side; pull your sewing yarn tightly and then stretch the seam gently. This helps to keep the seam as elastic as the knitting. Continue in this manner up to the armhole and then to the end of the Sleeve.

Fig. 37

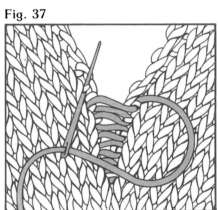

Vertical Weaving - A Half Stitch In

With **right** sides together and edges even, sew through both sides once to secure the beginning of the seam. Inserting needle from **right** to **left**, catch one strand from each edge *(Fig. 38)*. Inserting needle from **left** to **right** on next row, catch one strand from each edge.
Continue in this manner up to the armhole and then to the end of the Sleeve, being careful to match rows.

Fig. 38

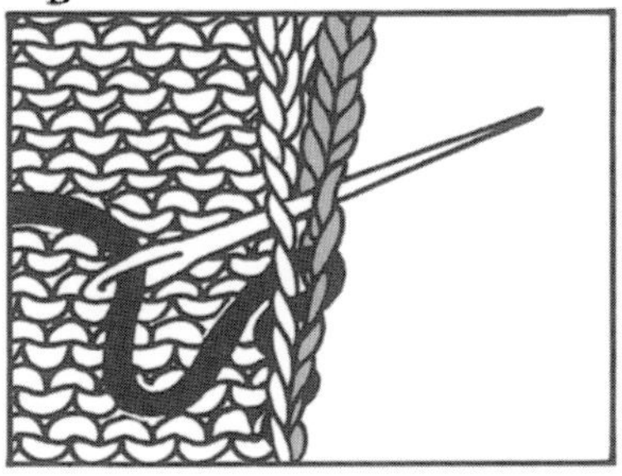

WHIPSTITCH

Whipstitch is not recommended for sewing seams. However, it is great for hems and attaching Collars because it is firm and it doesn't have the bulk of backstitch.
With **wrong** sides together, insert the needle from **right** to **left** through one strand on **each** piece *(Fig. 39)*. Bring the needle around and insert it from **right** to **left** through the next strand on both pieces.
Continue in this manner, keeping the sewing yarn fairly loose.

Fig. 39

GRAFTING

Grafting, or Kitchener Stitch, is a way of joining two sections horizontally, without a seam. The stitches are woven together directly from the needles. Both edges must have the same number of stitches.
There are two ways to position the pieces for grafting:
Lay both pieces on a table with **right** sides facing you *(Fig. 40)*, or hold both needles in the left hand with **wrong** sides together *(Fig. 41a)*.

Fig. 40

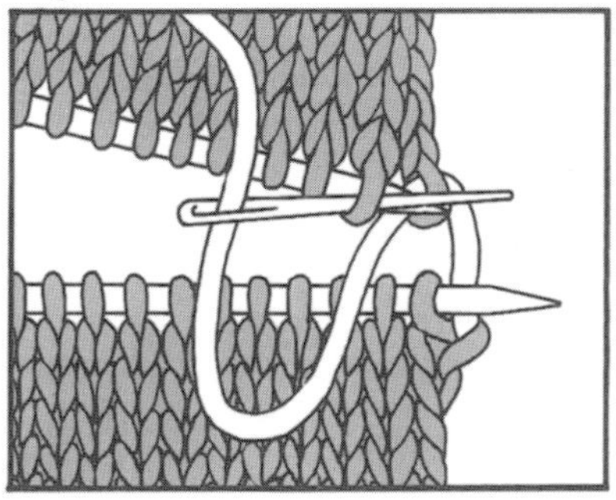

Cut the yarn on the front piece, leaving a long end, and thread a needle with this end.
Work in the following sequence, pulling the yarn through as if to **knit** or as if to **purl** with even tension, and keeping yarn under points of needles to avoid tangling and extra loops.

Stockinette Stitch
Step 1: Purl first stitch on **front** needle, leave on *(Fig. 41a)*.
Step 2: Knit first stitch on **back** needle, leave on *(Fig. 41b)*.
Step 3: Knit first stitch on **front** needle, slip off.
Step 4: Purl next stitch on **front** needle, leave on.
Step 5: Purl first stitch on **back** needle, slip off.
Step 6: Knit next stitch on **back** needle, leave on.
Repeat Steps 3-6 across until all stitches are worked off the needles.

Fig. 41a   **Fig. 41b**

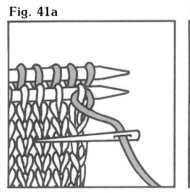

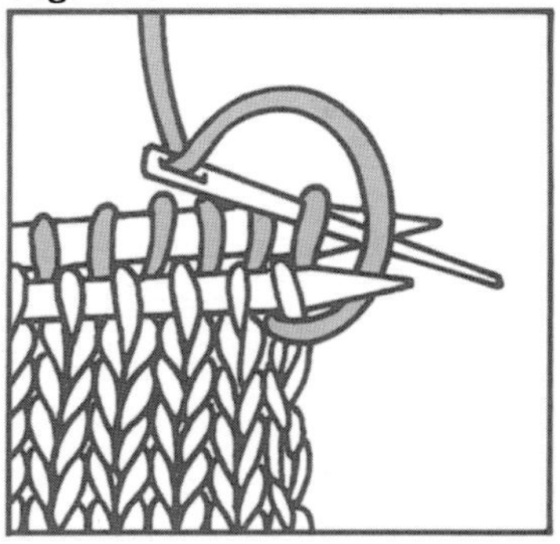

22

PICKING UP STITCHES

*"Picking up stitches along the finished edge of
a piece allows you to add ribbings, collars,
sleeves, and many other things without having
a seam."*

Picking up stitches leaves a small ridge on the opposite side.
Usually you will pick up stitches with the **right** side facing you,
so this ridge will be on the wrong side. If you are making a
collar that will turn down, it may lay nicer if you pick up the
stitches with the **wrong** side facing.
When instructed to pick up stitches, use one of the needles
and the yarn that you are going to continue working with.
Insert your knitting needle from the **front** to the **back** under
two strands at the edge of the worked piece **(Figs. 42a & b)**.
Put the yarn around the needle as if to **knit**, then bring the
needle with the yarn back through the stitch to the right side,
resulting in a stitch on the needle.
Repeat this along the edge.

Fig. 42a **Fig. 42b**

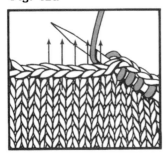 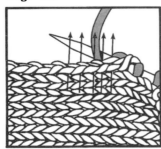

If you have a large number of stitches to pick up, you may
want to divide your work into quarters, marking the sections
with pins. You can then pick up a quarter of the total stitches
in each section. This will help keep your stitches even and well
spaced.

If the instructions do not tell you how many stitches to pick
up, follow this general rule:
Pick up one stitch in each stitch along a horizontal or bound
off edge and pick up three stitches in every four rows along a
vertical edge.
If it is easier, you may pick up stitches using a crochet hook,
sliding each one onto your knitting needle.

WEAVING IN YARN ENDS

*"Never, never tie a knot. They tend to poke
through to the right side and sometimes they
come untied and unravel. Then you have a
big problem. Resist the temptation to tie
knots. Weaving ends in is much safer and the
results are better."*

Turn your garment **wrong** side out.
If you started each new ball at the beginning of a row and left
your yarn ends long enough, this should be fairly easy.
Thread a yarn needle with the yarn end and weave it through
several stitches in the seam. If you don't think this is secure
enough, reverse directions and weave it back through 2 or 3
more stitches. Clip the yarn close to the work.
If you did join a new ball in mid-row, untie the temporary
knot, give the ends a half twist around each other, and weave
them in, either diagonally or horizontally. Be sure the yarn
doesn't "show" from the right side.

BLOCKING

*"Blocking sets the garment and smooths the
stitches to give your work a professional
appearance. I find it far more satisfactory to
block the assembled garment rather than
blocking the pieces before assembly."*

Before blocking, check the yarn label for any special
instructions. Some labels say, "Do not block". Many acrylics
and some blends may be damaged during blocking.
Note: Always use rust-proof pins.

On fragile acrylics that can be blocked, you simply pin your
garment to the correct size and cover it with dampened bath
towels. When the towels are dry, the garment is blocked.

If the garment is hand washable, carefully launder it using a
mild soap or detergent. Rinse it without wringing or twisting.
Remove any excess moisture by rolling it in a succession of
dry towels. If you prefer, you may put it in the final spin cycle
of your washer - but no water or heat, please. Lay the
garment on a large towel on a flat surface out of direct
sunlight. Using a tape measure, gently smooth and pat it to
the desired size and shape. When it is completely dry, it is
blocked.

Another method of blocking, that is especially good for wools,
requires a steam iron or a hand-held steamer. Turn the
garment **wrong** side out and pin it to the correct size. Hold the
steam iron or steamer just above the garment and steam it
thoroughly. Never let the weight of the iron touch your
garment because it will flatten the stitches. Never steam
ribbings, cables, or intricate raised patterns. Leave the garment
pinned until it is completely dry.

*"Whichever method you use, you will be
rewarded with a smooth, professional look."*

DUPLICATE STITCH

*"A duplicate stitch does just what it says - it
duplicates a stitch on your knitting.
It works beautifully for putting names on
Christmas stockings, monograms on sweaters,
or a small design on your knitting just because
you want to."*

Use a contrasting color of yarn threaded through a yarn
needle. Use the same weight yarn as you used in your
knitting. Be sure the contrasting color has the same care
instructions as the garment.

Each knit stitch forms a V and you want to completely cover
that V. Bring your needle up from the wrong side at the base
of the V, leaving a short end to be woven in later. Follow the
right side of the V up and insert the needle under the legs of
the V immediately above it **(Fig. 43a)**. Follow the left side of
the V back down to the base, and insert the needle where you
started this stitch **(Fig. 43b)**.
Repeat for all duplicate stitches, keeping tension even with
tension of knitted fabric to avoid puckering.
Duplicate stitch will cover best, if you change direction (right to
left and left to right) on alternate rows.

Fig. 43a **Fig. 43b**

 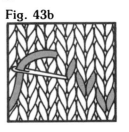

POM-POM

There are several commercial pom-pom makers available; however, there is a certain challenge in creating your own using either one of the following methods:

1. Cut two cardboard circles each 3″ in diameter. Cut a center hole ½″ in diameter in each circle. Thread a yarn needle with a doubled 72″ length of yarn.

   Holding the cardboard circles together and using additional lengths of yarn as needed, pass the needle through the center hole, over the outside edge, and through the center again *(Fig. 44a)* until the entire circle is covered.

   Cut the yarn between the edges of the two cardboard circles *(Fig. 44b)*.

   Slip an 18″ length of yarn between the cardboard circles; pull the yarn **tightly** around the center of the pom-pom and tie firmly *(Fig. 44c)*. Leave yarn ends long enough to attach the pom-pom.

   Remove the cardboard circles, fluff the pom-pom, and trim it into a smooth ball *(Fig. 44d)*.

Fig. 44a

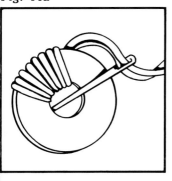

Fig. 44b

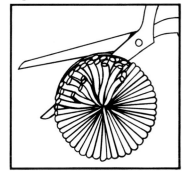

Fig. 44c

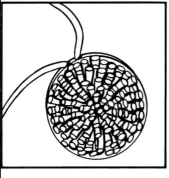

Fig. 44d

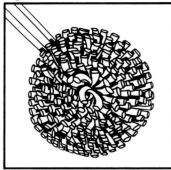

2. Cut a piece of cardboard 3″ wide and as long as you want the diameter of your finished pom-pom to be. Wind the yarn around the cardboard until it is approximately ½″ thick in the middle *(Fig. 45a)*.

   Carefully slip the yarn off of the cardboard and firmly tie an 18″ length of yarn around the middle *(Fig. 45b)*.

   Leave yarn ends long enough to attach the pom-pom. Cut the loops on both ends and trim the pom-pom into a smooth ball *(Fig. 44d)*.

Fig. 45a

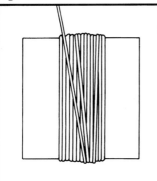

Fig. 45b

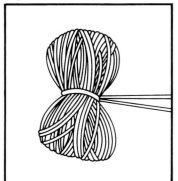

FRINGE

Cut a piece of cardboard 3″ wide and as long as you want your finished fringe to be. Wind the yarn **loosely** and **evenly** around the cardboard, then cut across one end when the card is filled; repeat as needed. Hold together half as many strands of yarn as needed for the finished fringe; fold in half.

With **wrong** side facing and using a crochet hook, draw the folded end up through a stitch and pull the loose ends through the folded end *(Fig. 46a)*; draw the knot up **tightly** *(Fig. 46b)*. Repeat as instructed. Lay piece flat on a hard surface and trim the ends.

Fig. 46a

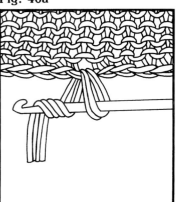

Fig. 46b

TASSEL

Cut a piece of cardboard 3″ wide and as long as you want your finished tassel to be. Wind a double strand of yarn around the cardboard approximately 20 times. Cut an 18″ length of yarn and insert it under all of the strands at the top of the cardboard; pull up **tightly** and tie securely. Leave the yarn ends long enough to attach the tassel. Cut the yarn at the opposite end of the cardboard *(Fig 47a)* and then remove it. Cut a 6″ length of yarn and wrap it **tightly** around the tassel twice, ½″ below the top *(Fig. 47b)*; tie securely. Trim the ends.

Fig. 47a

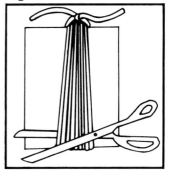

Fig. 47b

TWISTED CORD

Cut 2 pieces of yarn, each **3 times** as long as the desired finished length. Fasten one end to a stationary object **or** have another person hold it. Holding both pieces together, twist until **tight**. Fold in half and let it twist itself; knot both ends and cut the loops on the folded end.

KNITTED CORD

Using double pointed needles, cast on 3 sts.
★ K3, do **not** turn, slide the stitches to the opposite end of the needle; repeat from ★ until the cord measures the desired finished length. Bind off.

SINGLE CROCHET EDGING

A single crochet edging is an alternative finishing around a neckline or armholes. It gives the opening stability and provides a neat finished look.

LITTLE EXTRAS

"The lesson format is now complete and, if you have practiced each lesson carefully, you should be ready to choose your first pattern and knit one of the designs on pages 34 to 48.
But, please continue to read the next few pages. We have included several 'little extras' and have added some 'hints and tips' that will help you to perfect your new skill."

ONE NEEDLE (SLING SHOT) METHOD OF CASTING ON

"This method will give you a firm, elastic cast on edge and is the preferable way to begin any knitting. It looks complicated, but it isn't. Just remember that, with practice, this too will be easy for you to do."

Measure one inch of yarn for each stitch that you want to cast on (Example - 20 inches for 20 sts).
Now make a slip knot at that point.
Hold the needle with the slip knot in your right hand with your index finger resting on the slip knot.
With the yarn end forward and the working yarn behind, insert your left thumb and index finger between these two strands, holding both strands with your remaining 3 fingers *(Photo FF)*.
Bring your left hand up, moving your thumb and index finger apart *(Photo GG)*.

★ Insert the needle from the bottom into the thumb loop *(Photo HH)*, then down into the index finger loop *(Photo II)*, pulling it through the thumb loop *(Photo JJ)*.
Slip your thumb out of the loop and tighten your new stitch by inserting your thumb back between the two strands *(Photo KK)* and moving your thumb and index finger apart, ready to begin the next stitch just as you did in *Photo GG*.

Photo FF

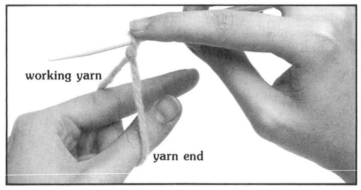

Photo II

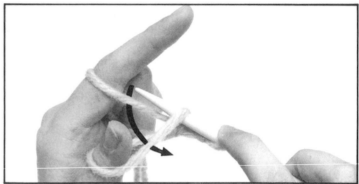

Photo GG

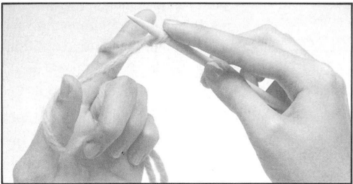

Photo JJ

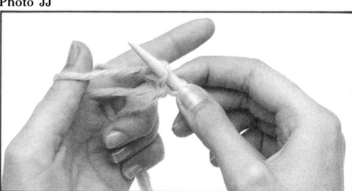

Photo HH

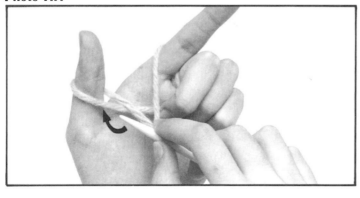

Photo KK

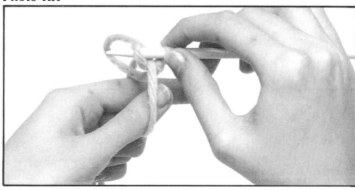

"You did that so well !!! Try it again from the ★. That wasn't nearly as complicated as it sounds ... or looks. However, this is one of those things that we all tend to forget because we don't use it on a daily basis. A quick review will make you an expert again, and some morning you'll get out of bed knowing how to cast on without reviewing it.
Feel free to paste a gold star on your calendar that day."

When you knit a tube, as for a skirt, hat, sock, or mitten, you are going to work around and around on the outside of the circle, with the **right** side of the knitting facing you.
If your piece is Stockinette Stitch, you have eliminated having to work any purl rows, and you will knit *every round*.
If your piece is Garter Stitch, alternate one knit round with one purl round.

CIRCULAR NEEDLE

Cast on all the stitches.
Now, inspect the cast on row to be sure that the cast on ridge lays on the inside of the needle at all times and **never** rolls around the needle *(Fig. 48)*.
If it does, straighten it out immediately.
Hold the needle so that the ball of yarn is attached to the stitch closest to the right hand point.
Place a marker on the right hand point to mark the beginning of the rounds.
Knit the stitches on the left hand point.

Fig. 48

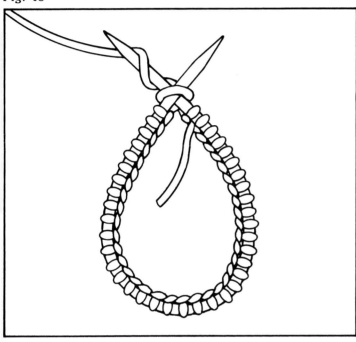

Continue knitting around and around **without turning the work**; but, for the first three rounds or so, check to be sure that the cast on edge has not twisted around the needle. If it has, it is impossible to untwist it. The only way to fix this is to rip it out and return to the cast on row.

Cast all of the stitches onto one needle. Then slip one third of them onto a second needle and one third of them onto a third needle *(Fig. 49a)*.
Now, form a triangle of the three needles with the ball of yarn attached to the stitch closest to the tip of the needle at the top right of the triangle. All cast on ridges should lay on the inside of the triangle. Do **not** twist the cast on ridge.
With the fourth needle, knit across the stitches on the first needle *(Fig. 49b)*. After you have knit all the stitches off the first needle onto the fourth needle, you will now have an empty needle with which to knit the stitches from the next needle. Work the first stitch of each needle firmly to prevent gaps.
Continue in this manner, knitting around and around, checking occasionally, for at least the first three rounds, to be sure that your cast on edge has not twisted around any of the needles.

Fig. 49a

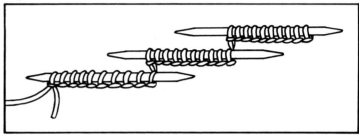

Fig. 49b

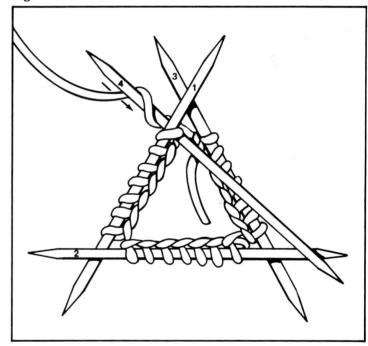

"There are many methods of making buttonholes; below you'll find the three that are most generally used."

YO BUTTONHOLE

This is the simplest of all and is used most frequently in baby clothes, because it makes a small hole **(Photo LL)**.
It is worked as follows: YO, K2 tog.

Photo LL

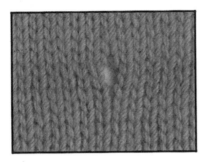

TWO ROW BUTTONHOLE

This is perhaps the most popular. On Buttonhole Row 1, work to the desired position of the buttonhole, bind off the required number of stitches and complete the row. On Row 2, work to the bound off stitches, turn your work around, cast on the same number of stitches that you bound off, turn your work again and complete the row **(Photo MM)**.
Embroidery (Buttonhole Stitch) is sometimes added to the completed garment for a more finished look.

Photo MM

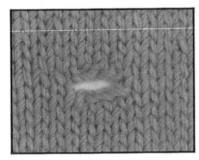

VERTICAL BUTTONHOLE

This one is neat and tidy. Both sides of the buttonhole are worked at the same time, using separate yarn. Wind a small ball of yarn. Work across the body of the garment with the working yarn to the desired position of the buttonhole; drop this yarn and work the last few stitches with the small ball. Continue in this manner, working the stitches from the front edge to the buttonhole with the small ball and working the stitches from the body of the garment with the working yarn, for the number of rows instructed; cut the small ball. Then, work across all the stitches on the next row with the working yarn **(Photo NN)**. This buttonhole rarely needs any additional finishing.

Photo NN

"OK, now the garment is complete, but you've decided you want a pocket right there, just to carry your handkerchief. Don't panic; we're going to tell you how to put it there. Also, we're going to tell you about a few of the many kinds of pockets you can make."

FALSE POCKET

This is a strip or a band that is sewn to the sweater to give the appearance of a pocket opening.

PATCH POCKET

This is knit separately and sewn to the outside of the finished sweater.

SIDE SEAM POCKET

This is knit separately and sewn into an opening on the side seam.

INSET POCKET

This is knit before beginning the Front of the sweater and placed on a stitch holder. When you reach the place on the Front where you want the opening of the pocket to be, bind off the same number of stitches as the pocket and continue working across the row. On the next row, when you reach the bound off stitches, work across the stitches on the stitch holder, then continue working across the row. The bound off stitches can later be picked up and worked in ribbing, garter stitch, or in just plain stockinette stitch (folded and hemmed) to form the band.

CABLES

*"Making Cables is one of those knitting techniques that impresses your friends and family, but is really easy to do.
Relax, I'm not about to tell your friends and family that it is easy, I'm only telling you."*

To try one:
Cast on 18 sts **loosely**.
Row 1: K4, P2, K6, P2, K4.
Row 2: P4, K2, P6, K2, P4.
Row 3: K4, P2, slip the next 3 sts onto a cable needle as if to **purl** and hold them **behind** your work **(Fig. 50a)**. Knit the next 3 sts on the left needle. Now, knit the 3 sts from the cable needle onto your right needle, being sure that the first st you knit is the first one you slipped onto the cable needle **(Fig. 50b)**, P2, K4.
Row 4: P4, K2, P6, K2, P4.
Row 5: K4, P2, K6, P2, K4.
Row 6: P4, K2, P6, K2, P4.

Fig. 50a　　　　　**Fig. 50b**

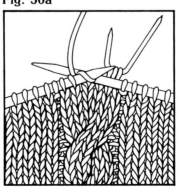
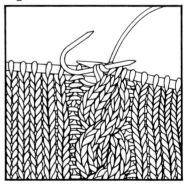

*"That's really good! Now do all 6 rows again. Aren't you delighted? I am!
There are many varieties of cable stitches, but the basic technique is the same. Now, you are able to do any and all of them. You might even want to walk around your block and show everyone what you've just accomplished!"*

COLOR KNITTING

STRAND KNITTING

"This is the method of knitting that uses two colors in the same row, as in one of those magnificent Norwegian ski sweaters."

This method includes Fair Isle, Norwegian, Scandinavian, and Shetland knitting and usually involves changing colors every few stitches in one row. The yarn not being used is carried across the wrong side of the knitting. The finished piece will be smooth and elastic, if the yarn being carried is neither too tight nor too loose. Spread your stitches on the needle so that you will have the correct tension on the yarn that is being carried. If the yarn must be carried for more than 3 stitches, it should be secured. There are diffent ways to do this:

1. Drop the color you are using, lay the other color to your left on top of it, pick up the color you were using and continue working. You have formed a little shelf that the other color will lay on *(Fig. 51)*. As you get close to the end of the row, it will become more and more apparent that your two balls of yarn are becoming very, very twisted. You may stop and untwist them as often as you like; or, if you wait for the purl row, they will untwist themselves.

Fig. 51

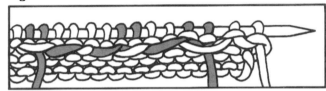

2. Hold the yarn that is predominant in your right hand and the other color in your left hand. When working a **knit** row, go in the next stitch as you always do. Lay the strand of yarn in your left hand between the needles from the right to left *(Fig. 52a)*; now, complete your stitch as you normally would, without bringing the extra strand through to the right side. This strand will be secured after you work your next stitch.
Fig. 52b illustrates this same technique on a purl row.
This process is a bit more difficult to learn, but a lot easier to do, because the tension on the yarn being carried is easier to control and you are not twisting the yarns.

Fig. 52a

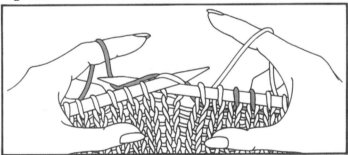

Fig. 52b

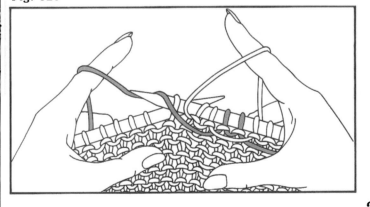

BOBBIN KNITTING

"This is another one of those things that looks incredibly difficult, but isn't. You use bobbins when you are knitting argyle patterns or children's sweaters with little white angora bunnies on them."

In Intarsia knitting, better known as Bobbin knitting, there are usually large areas of color. Bobbins are used to hold the small amount of yarn needed to work each color change and also to help keep the different colored yarns from tangling. You'll need to wind a bobbin for each color change, using as many bobbins as necessary to avoid carrying the yarn across the back.
Start each bobbin as you would a new ball of yarn *(see Hints and Tips, page 29)*, leaving a 6" end to weave in later. Always keep the bobbins on the wrong side of your work and only unfasten enough yarn to work the area comfortably, otherwise they too will tangle.

CHANGING COLORS

When changing colors, always pick up the new color yarn from **beneath** the dropped yarn and keep the color which has just been worked to the left *(Fig. 53)*. This will avoid holes in the finished piece. Take extra care to keep your tension even.

Fig. 53

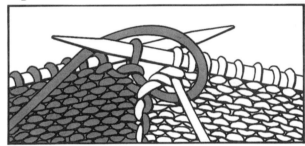

FOLLOWING A CHART

Designs for Bobbin knitting and Strand knitting are usually worked from a chart. The chart shows each stitch as a square, indicating what color each stitch should be. Always follow a chart from bottom to top, reading it from right to left on the right side rows, and from left to right on the wrong side rows. If you are knitting in rounds on a circular needle or on double pointed needles, always read the chart from right to left.

Continued on page 29.

CHANGING COLOR IN RIBBING

"I'll share a little secret with you - one that most knitters are not aware of and even garment manufacturers don't seem to know."

When working a striped ribbing, little "nubs" of color appear on the right side **(Photo OO)**. To eliminate those unsightly "nubs" and improve the overall appearance of your garment, always knit across the **first** row of **each** color change and continue in ribbing as before **(Photo PP)**.

Photo OO   wrong

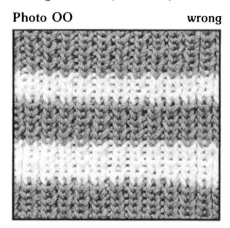

Photo PP   right

Note: Ribbings have been stretched to show detail.

"What? Knit across in the middle of my ribbing! Yes, don't be afraid to experiment - it works! The knit rows will not affect the elasticity of the ribbing."

However, there are exceptions:
1. This technique only works when each stripe consists of an even number of rows of 2 or more rows.
   Photo PP shows a 6 row and a 4 row contrasting color stripe.
2. If the stripes are an odd number of rows (Example - 3, 5, 7) you would **purl** across when working a **wrong** side row and **knit** across when working a **right** side row.

"Try these methods on a small piece of ribbing and see the results for yourself. I know that you'll be impressed. Isn't it fun to learn new techniques?"

CHANGING COLOR IN GARTER STITCH

Most patterns that use color changes in garter stitch will tell you on which row (a **right** side row or a **wrong** side row) to change colors. But, if you are being creative on your own, always change colors on a **right** side row to prevent those unsightly little "nubs" of color from showing.

HINTS AND TIPS

"As an added bonus, let's peek inside my 'bag of tricks'. Some of these hints and tips are my own tried and true favorites. Others I've gathered over the years from fellow knitters and editors. All of them will help you gain confidence and become more professional in you knitting. Feel free to check back here anytime you need a little extra help. Remember, the main difference between the amateur and the professional is usually her 'little bag of tricks'."

DYE LOTS

Yarn is dyed in "lots" and then numbered. Different lots of the same color will vary slightly in shade and will be noticeable if knit in the same piece. Always buy enough yarn of the same dye lot to complete a project. Dye lots can never be matched exactly again.

If you absolutely must use two different dye lots, make an entire piece, such as a sleeve, or work all the ribbings with the different dye lot.

If you are really desperate, (and all of us are occasionally) try working two rows with the old and two rows with the new lot for about 2 inches. Keep doing this until your odd lot is knit into the garment. This blending is so subtle that the human eye won't believe what it sees.

WINDING YARN INTO A BALL

Most yarns come in ready to use "pull-skeins", where the yarn is pulled from the center of the skein. In this form, it is easy to keep clean and less likely to unwind too quickly or tangle. Some yarns, however, are sold in hanks which must be wound into balls before they are ready to use. Remove the label and unfold the skein to form a circle. Slip the yarn over the back of a chair and cut the knot that holds the strands together. Tie one end of the yarn **loosely** around your wrist. Gently wrap the yarn around two fingers until a small ball is formed. Remove your fingers and continue to wind the yarn **very loosely**, rotating to keep the ball uniform.

The yarn attached to your wrist will be the pull-out part of the skein. Take care to wind the ball **loosely**. If the yarn is pulled too tightly or stretched when wound, it will lose some of its elasticity.

JOINING A NEW BALL OF YARN

The best way to join yarn is to always join at the beginning of a row - not in the middle of a row. The joining will then end up in a seam and will not be visible on the finished garment. If you have four times the width of the piece you are knitting, you have enough yarn to work another row. Finish one row and cut that yarn leaving a 6″ end. Begin the next row with the new ball of yarn, leaving a 6″ end to weave in later.

If you leave the yarn ends long enough, the stitches will not come undone and you do not need to tie a knot. However, if you wish, you may tie a **temporary** single knot, that will later be untied and woven into the seam.

Sometimes your rows don't have a beginning or an end - as when you are knitting a tube for a skirt, sock, mitten, or hat. When this happens, leave a 6″ end of the old yarn and begin knitting with the new ball of yarn. Again, you may tie a **temporary** single knot.

Sometimes there will be a knot in your ball of yarn. It is **not** meant to be preserved. The knot should be cut out and the yarn should be joined as if it were a new ball.

SEAM-SEWING YARN

When beginning or ending a piece of knitting, if you leave a long yarn end, you should have enough to sew the seam without having to join another piece, eliminating the need to weave in any extra yarn ends.

RIBBING

As a general rule, instructions are written for K1, P1 ribbing to be worked over an even number of stitches. When written this way, you would always begin each row with a knit stitch. However, if you can recognize your stitches easily *(see page 7)* and if you intend to weave the side seams, the seam will be neater if the bottom ribbing is worked on an odd number of stitches.

Feel free to subtract one stitch from the cast on, work the ribbing for the required length, and increase that one stitch just before you begin the body of the garment.

RIGHT AND WRONG SIDE OF CAST ON

Most beginners and even some experienced knitters are not aware that there is a difference in the sides of the cast on row. Two pieces of basic ribbing have been photographed to illustrate the difference. **Photo QQ** is an example of the **wrong** side; **Photo RR**, the **right** side. Notice the smooth edge in **Photo RR** as compared to **Photo QQ**.

Once the ribbing has been worked to the desired length and before beginning the pattern stitch of the piece (in this example we've used Stockinette Stitch), take a moment to examine the cast on before beginning that first pattern row.

This is the time to decide whether to begin with a knit row or with a purl row, in order to have the right side of the cast on edge match the knit side of your garment.

If working a more involved pattern in the body, read the pattern rows to find out whether the even numbered rows or the odd numbered rows are the right side. You may have to work one more row of ribbing before beginning the pattern, but that little bit of extra effort will result in a garment that is more professional in appearance.

Photo QQ   **wrong**

Photo RR   **right**

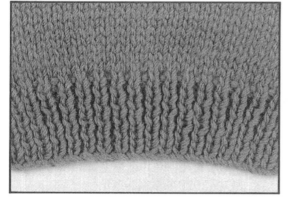

CHANGING NEEDLES

Most instructions call for the use of smaller size needles for the ribbing. This is to ensure a snug, elastic fit.

If you had to change to different size needles to obtain correct gauge when you made your gauge swatch, be sure to change the smaller size needles accordingly - generally two sizes smaller than those used for the body.

After the ribbing, the instructions will tell you to change to larger size needles. To do this, replace the needle in your right hand with the larger size needle and work the next row. Continue knitting with both larger size needles.

INCREASING EVENLY ACROSS THE ROW

When the directions state "increase a number of stitches evenly across the row", most of us seem to come to a halt.

How do we figure what even is? . . . especially if it doesn't quite work out! There are probably as many ways to arrive at the answer as there are individual knitters.

Here is one method that works:

To increase evenly across a row, add one to the number of increases required and divide that number into the number of stitches on the needle. The result is the number of stitches to be worked between each increase.

This method eliminates the increase stitch at the beginning and end of a row, creating a smooth line for sewing the seam. Generally, this rule works; however, it is sometimes necessary to work less stitches between increases to arrive at the correct **total** number of stitches. Remember, the important point is to reach that total, with the increases spaced as evenly as possible.

EXAMPLE

54 stitches to be increased by 6 evenly = total 60

$6 + 1 = 7$ $54 \div 7 = 7$ **(closest)**

Work 7 stitches between increases

$7 \times 7 = 49$ space stitches
$6 \times 2 = \underline{12}$ increases
61 **total**

Eliminate the 1 extra stitch in the center

7 ● 7 ● 7 ● 6 ● 7 ● 7 ● 7
   (60 stitches total)

● = increase stitch = 2 stitches

ROW GAUGE

Many times a piece is worked only to inches and, if your row gauge is not exact, your work will turn out fine.

However, row gauge is very important in some designs, especially raglans, where the armhole depth and sleeve cap length are determined entirely by rows, or in designs with intricate pattern stitches, where the overall length of the piece is obtained by a specific repeat of the pattern rows.

When knitting one of these designs and you are able to obtain stitch gauge in your swatch but your row gauge is slightly off, it can be corrected by using a different size needle on alternate rows, without affecting your stitch gauge.

If you have more rows per inch than specified, use a larger size needle on the purl rows; if you have fewer rows per inch, use a smaller size needle on the purl rows. Keep trying until you find just the right combination that will give you both stitch gauge **and** row gauge. DO NOT HESITATE TO CHANGE NEEDLE SIZE TO OBTAIN CORRECT GAUGE.

MULTIPLES

A multiple is the number of stitches needed to complete one repeat of a pattern stitch.

For instance, K2, P2 ribbing is a multiple of four, because it takes four stitches to repeat the pattern. Therefore, the number of stitches on the needle must be divisible by four. This information is usually given at the beginning of a pattern. Some multiples might also specify the number of rows required to complete the pattern.

For instance, a lace pattern could have a multiple of 8 stitches plus 1 stitch, with a 12 row repeat.

MEASURING TIPS

When measuring your knitting, do not include the needle. Always use a ruler or a yardstick; do not use a measuring tape.

Place your ruler just below the needle for an accurate measurement.

When measuring the armhole depth, do not measure around the curve. If you measure around the curve, your armhole will be too shallow.

It's a good idea to attach a small piece of contrasting color yarn to a stitch in the middle of the first bind off row (the start of the armhole). Then measure from the needle to this mark to determine the depth.

WORKING BOTH SIDES OF NECK AT THE SAME TIME

Not all patterns give instructions for working both sides of the neck at the same time. However, it is much better to do so and it almost guarantees that both sides will be the same length.

When instructions are written for both sides to be worked at the same time, the **semicolon** (;) is the signal for you to drop your first yarn and begin working with the second yarn.

EXAMPLE
Neck Shaping
Note: Both sides of Neck are worked at the same time, using separate yarn for each side.
Row 1: Work across 25 sts, slip 15 sts onto st holder; with second yarn, work across: 25 sts **each** side.
Row 2: Work across; work across.
Row 3 (Decrease row): Work across to within 2 sts of Neck edge, decrease; decrease, work across: 24 sts **each** side.

IMPORTANT: Do not lay your work down with one piece on each needle. If you do, it will be difficult to determine which side you worked last.

When instructions state to shape right side, then, "work left side same as right side, reversing all shaping", it will be easier for you to work both sides at the same time. This way, you will know exactly when to decrease and all your rows will match.

WORKING BOTH SLEEVES AT THE SAME TIME

Yes, you may knit both sleeves at the same time.
Each sleeve will have its own ball of yarn, just the same as working both sides of the neck at the same time. This method can also be used for both front sides of a cardigan. Many knitters prefer this method because it guarantees that both pieces will be the same length.

BINDING OFF TIPS

It takes two stitches to bind off one stitch. Count each stitch as you bind it off, not as you knit it.

BINDING OFF IN PATTERN
Unless otherwise stated, when you are instructed to bind off your stitches, you should always bind off in pattern. In reality, you are working another row. Whether your bind off is at the shoulders, the back of the neck, or around the neck or armhole ribbing, your work will be more professional in appearance, if the bind off row is in pattern.
If you are knitting, knit the stitches as you bind off.
If you are purling, purl the stitches as you bind off.
If you are doing both, knit the knit stitches and purl the purl stitches as you bind off.
When binding off in ribbing, this is extremely important.
Binding off in pattern maintains the elasticity of the ribbing.

BINDING OFF LOOSELY VERSUS TIGHTLY
Bind off loosely for an edge with elasticity and bind off tightly for a firm edge.
Nothing is more frustrating than completing a sweater and not being able to get it over your head. So, when binding off a crew neck or a turtle neck ribbing, always bind off **loosely**. The bound off stitches should stretch as much as the ribbing does. To make this easier, replace the needle in your right hand with a larger size needle.
To guarantee that the shoulders of your garment will always stay firmly in place and will not sag or droop, always bind off **tightly**.
Bind off tightly when using cotton yarn, because of its tendency to stretch.

SMOOTH BIND OFF EDGE
To eliminate a square or stair-step effect when working sleeve or shoulder bind-offs, begin each bind-off row with a decrease, binding off one less stitch. A smoother, more rounded edge will result.

PLACING BUTTONS

When marking the front band of a Cardigan for buttons, it is important to remember that there is one less space between them than there are buttons (7 buttons = 6 spaces) and sometimes the last button will be placed on the Neck Ribbing.

EXAMPLE
Mark Front Band for 7 buttons, having first button ½" above lower edge and last button on the Neck Ribbing.
Using a pin or a contrasting color yarn, mark the first and the last button, then measure the distance between them and divide this measurement by 6. The result is the distance between each remaining button *(Fig. 54)*.

Fig. 54

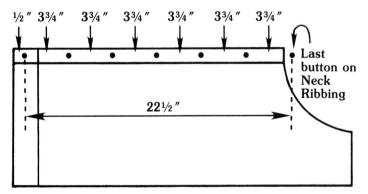

By knitting the button band first and marking the button placement carefully, you can now knit the buttonhole band and feel confident when spacing the buttonholes.

WHAT TO DO ABOUT KNITTING THAT HAS BEEN SITTING

If your knitting has been left on the needle for several weeks without working on it, that yarn has totally conformed to the needle. If you just continue to knit, there will always be a distinguishable line in your knitting. This will annoy you long after you have finished the piece.

To avoid this, it's a good idea to rip back one row and throw that yarn away.

If you know ahead of time that it will be awhile before you can knit again, slip the stitches onto a smaller size needle or onto the nylon cable of a circular needle. This will prevent damage to the yarn and enable you to continue knitting without ripping.

REUSING YARN

If you have ripped out a large piece of your knitting and want to reuse the yarn, it's a good idea to remove the crinkles that have formed.

To do this, wind the yarn around a large box, such as a suit box. Tie it in four places with a contrasting color yarn and remove the hank from the box.

If you have a microwave, boil a bowl of water, turn off the microwave, and lay the hank of yarn beside the bowl. Leave it in the microwave for about 20 minutes. This should remove the crinkles.

If you don't have a microwave, hold the hank over the steaming spout of a tea kettle for several minutes, taking care not to burn yourself. Shake the hank a bit to help remove the crinkles.

Either way, lay the hank flat on a towel and allow to dry completely. Then wind it **loosely** into a ball.

USING COTTON OR SILK YARN

Because cotton and silk yarns have limited elasticity, they tend to expand with body heat and a garment knit with these yarns will stretch. You will be more pleased with the fit of your garment, if you make the size closest to your actual body size. Cotton yarn doesn't slide through your fingers the same way that acrylic or wool yarns do, making it harder to control your tension. Since the slightest variation in tension results in uneven stitches, you should practice with this yarn first, before beginning your garment, to get accustomed to the "feel" of the yarn.

KNITTING WITH ELASTIC THREAD

Elastic thread comes in different colors, weights, sizes, and packaging.

Some are very fine and are meant to be held right along with your yarn, when knitting waistbands, collars or cuffs, to prevent sagging or stretching.

Others are just a bit heavier but can still be used to prevent sagging or stretching by catching the thread in each knit stitch of K1, P1 ribbing *(see Strand Knitting, page 28)* on every fourth row.

To do this, use a single strand, or a double strand for added strength, leaving a 6" end at each side. When the garment is complete, adjust the elastic to the correct size and tie the corresponding ends together, weaving them into the seams. Since many colors are available, this thread can even be added to a finished garment, enabling you to correct a ribbing that has lost its elasticity.

Thread a needle with the elastic thread and, working on the wrong side, weave it through half of each knit stitch. Leave a 6" end at the beginning and at the end of each row, adjust the elastic, and tie the ends, weaving them into the side seam. Do this at the bottom edge, just below the body at the top edge, and space any remaining rows of elastic about ½" apart.

STRAIGHTENING CIRCULAR NEEDLES

Occasionally, the nylon cable between the working ends of a circular needle is stiff and curled. Soaking the needle in a pan of very hot water for a few minutes will uncurl the cable and return its flexibility.

EASIER SLEEVE SEAMS

When Sleeve increases and decreases are worked one stitch in from each edge, they will show on the finished garment, but the seam will be much easier to weave because both edges will be smooth.

EXAMPLE
Right Side Row: K1, increase, work across to last 2 sts, increase, K1.

SELVAGE STITCHES

1. If one stitch is added to each side of your work, the final finishing of your garment will be easier.

   ### EXAMPLE
   When working an all-over lace pattern, if one extra stitch at **each** edge is worked in Stockinette Stitch, the seams will be easier to weave.

2. When working a Garter Stitch Border, a selvage stitch will provide a smooth edge.
   Work as follows:
   With yarn forward, slip the first stitch on **each** row as if to **purl** and knit the **last** stitch on each row.

STITCH HOLDERS

When instructed to slip a group of stitches onto a stitch holder, always slip them as if to **purl**, to prevent twisted stitches. Later, when it is time to work them again, they will be in the correct position.

ZIPPERS

Instead of working a buttonhole band on a cardigan, a zipper can be added instead.

With the **right** side of the garment facing and taking care not to stretch the knitting, pin the zipper into the opening, leaving the "teeth" exposed. Baste in place. Backstitch the zipper to the garment close to the edge of the knitting, using matching thread.

ABOUT THE AUTHOR

Evie was the only child of Sam ("Doc") and Ann Cohen. Doc was a dentist in Wausau, a small city surrounded by Wisconsin's dairy farms. He graduated from dental school a year before he was legally old enough to practice independently. Her mother, Ann, received a degree in Home Economics and was one of the original Betty Crockers, traveling throughout the Midwest giving cooking demonstrations. That was in the early 1920's, a time when few women worked outside the home, not to mention traveled alone. The message those two high achievers gave their only child was the conviction that a girl, particularly their daughter, could do anything she set her mind to doing.

Evie's introduction to knitting came at the age of seven, when her cousin taught her to make a garter stitch headband. Later, when she was in junior high school, Evie discovered that knitting was one of the "in" activities among teenage girls. She announced that she wanted to make a sweater, but her mother refused to buy the yarn unless Evie first learned to knit a pair of socks. By the time she had produced a pair of ankle socks with cables, she knew how to cast on, purl, increase, decrease and bind off. Her mother kept her end of the bargain and Evie's first sweater was a red set-in-sleeve pullover which she made on circular needles. She got lots of practice knitting throughout high school, making sweaters for her family and friends as well as several she made for soldiers overseas, with yarn supplied by the Red Cross.

Evie entered the University of Wisconsin and took courses in knitting, sewing and art, as well as in psychology and physiology as part of her training to become an Occupational Therapist. When she was a junior, she was introduced to Irv Rosen at her roommate's wedding. When Evie graduated the following year, they became engaged and were married after she completed her internship in New York.

Irv owned a grocery store in Atlanta, so the newlyweds settled in his hometown. While there, Evie worked with handicapped children, also in a private psychiatric hospital, and later for the Veteran's Administration. After 6 years in Atlanta, they decided to move back to Wausau, taking with them their 4 year old daughter, Robbin. Their son Mike was born shortly after they arrived and soon Evie was back at work - this time at the local tuberculosis sanatorium, where she remained employed even after it had become a geriatric facility.

In 1964 Evie and her friend, Joy, opened *The Knitting Nook* in a converted double garage. Evie was the knitting instructor and Joy the business manager of the team. After 3 years their merchandise had expanded from just yarn to include needlepoint and crewel, so they moved the shop to its much larger and present location. Later, Joy retired, because of ill health, and sold her share of *The Knitting Nook* to Evie.

Evie began her career as a designer when a dress she and Joy had designed together was purchased by the Spinnerin Yarn Co. Since that time, Evie has designed original patterns for publication in McCall's Needlework and Workbasket magazines and in books or leaflets produced by Brunswick, American School of Needlework, Bucilla, Bates, Spinnerin, Kappie Originals, and Berry Patch. Alone, **Leisure Arts** has published 20 leaflets containing her designs.

Evie served as president of the American Professional Needlework Retailers (APNR) from 1973 to 1975, during which time plans were laid for the teacher certification program. She has taught the intermediate knitting classes for the certification program since 1981 and has continued her teaching at her shop, at the YWCA Adult Education Program, the Adult Education Department of the North Central Technical Institute in Wausau, and has recently begun teaching at the Knitting Guild of America's annual national convention.

In addition to her membership in APNR, Evie belongs to The Knitting Guild of America, Southeastern Yarncrafters Guild, and was recently elected as the first retailer to serve on the board of The National Needlework Association. She also finds time for various religious, civic, and philanthropic organizations.

"I do one thing in this world really well; I knit." So says our author Evie Rosen and if she believes that is all she does well, she's selling herself very short. She has been directly responsible for teaching thousands of students and by teaching teachers, she has indirectly influenced tens of thousands more. She has taught beginner and advanced knitters as well as children and retirees in nursing homes. And she has taught them in every conceivable atmosphere - her home, her shop, in hospitals, at the YWCA, and at Purdue University. Her love of her craft and her enthusiasm have infected every student. Her warmth and her patience have encouraged and given confidence to even the most apprehensive. And nothing gives her more joy than seeing her students fall in love with something that has given her so much pleasure and has been such an important part of her life.

CONGRATULATIONS!
This is Graduation Day.

All of the information needed to complete the following designs has been included in this leaflet. Therefore, if you come to an unfamiliar term while working a design, please refer to the Index, page 49, for direction.

The skill level needed for the designs ranges from beginner to intermediate.
We recommend the Slipper, Hat and Scarf Set, or the Garter Stitch Vest as good first projects for the beginning knitter.

As your skills and confidence increase, you will want something more challenging, such as the Baby Afghan, Pullover, Sampler Vest, or the Hooded Baby Jacket.

Just remember:
Read the instructions carefully, use the Lessons for guidance, and most important of all - relax and enjoy your knitting !

HAT & SCARF
Instructions on page 37

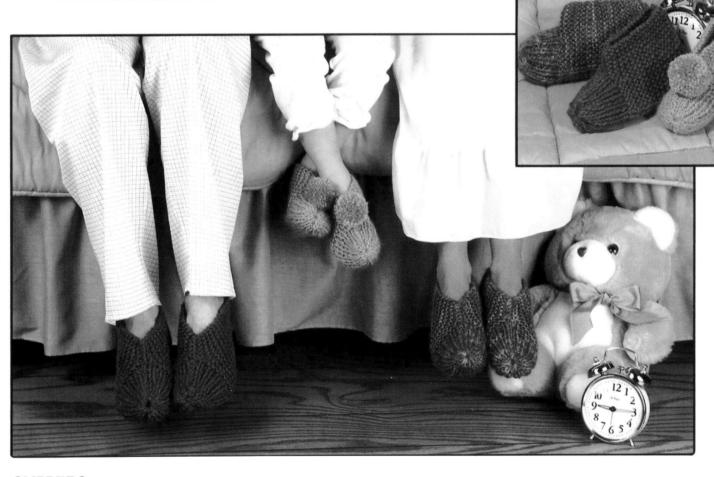

SLIPPERS
Instructions on page 37

36

HAT

Photograph on page 35.

Size: One size fits all

MATERIALS

Worsted Weight Brushed Acrylic Yarn, approximately:
   Main Color - 2 ounces, (60 grams, 155 yards)
   Color A - 1½ ounces, (40 grams, 115 yards)
   Color B - 1½ ounces, (40 grams, 115 yards)
   Note: If using a basic worsted weight yarn, increase ounces and grams by ¼ or purchase yarn according to yardage.
Straight knitting needles, size 17 (12.00 mm) **or** size needed for gauge
Yarn needle

GAUGE: Holding double strand of yarn,
      In Stockinette Stitch, 8 sts and 13 rows = 4″

Note: Entire Hat is worked holding two strands of yarn together.

Stripe Sequence

   4 rows Color A
   6 rows Color B
   4 rows Color A
   8 rows Main Color

With Main Color, cast on 40 sts **loosely**.
Work 8 rows in Stockinette Stitch (knit one row, purl one row).
Continuing in Stockinette Stitch, work Stripe Sequence 3 times.
Cut Main Color, leaving an 18″ end.

FINISHING

Thread a yarn needle with the end and separately slip each stitch from the knitting needle onto the yarn, gathering the stitches tightly.
Secure end.
Weave seam *(Fig. 37, page 22)*.
Weave in all yarn ends.
Gather opposite end of Hat and secure.
Insert first gathered end inside the Hat to meet second gathered end and tack in place.
Fold to form brim.

SCARF

Photograph on page 35.

Finished Size: 7″ x 40″ before fringe

MATERIALS

Worsted Weight Brushed Acrylic Yarn, approximately:
   Main Color - 2 ounces, (60 grams, 155 yards)
   Color A - 1½ ounces, (40 grams, 115 yards)
   Color B - 1½ ounces, (40 grams, 115 yards)
   Note: If using a basic worsted weight yarn, increase ounces and grams by ¼ or purchase yarn according to yardage.
Straight knitting needles, size 13 (9.00 mm) **or** size needed for gauge
Yarn needle

GAUGE: In Stockinette Stitch, 12 sts and 16 rows = 4″

With Main Color, cast on 44 sts **loosely**.
Work 8 rows in Stockinette Stitch (knit one row, purl one row).
Continuing in Stockinette Stitch, work Hat Stripe Sequence 7 times.
Bind off all sts **loosely**.

FINISHING

Weave seam *(Fig. 37, page 22)*.
Weave in all yarn ends.

FRINGE

Flatten Scarf with seam at center back.
Using Main Color, add Fringe *(Figs. 46a & b, page 24)* evenly across each end, working through **both** thicknesses.
Lay Scarf flat on a hard surface and trim ends.

SLIPPERS

Photograph on page 35.

Sizes:	Small	Medium	Large
Sole Length:	7″	8½″	10″

Size Note: Instructions are written for size Small with sizes Medium and Large in parentheses. Instructions will be easier to read, if you circle all the numbers pertaining to your size.

MATERIALS

Bulky Weight Yarn, approximately:
   5(5½-6) ounces, [140(160-170) grams, 125(135-150) yards]
Straight knitting needles, size 10 (6.00 mm) **or** size needed for gauge
Yarn needle

GAUGE: In Garter Stitch, 14 sts and 24 rows = 4″

Cast on 39 sts **loosely**.
Row 1: K 14, P1, K9, P1, K 14.
Row 2 (Right side)**:** Knit across.
Repeat Rows 1 and 2 for pattern until piece measures approximately 4(5½-7)″, ending by working Row 2.
TOE
Row 1: Bind off 5 sts, K8, P1, K9, P1, K 14: 34 sts.
Row 2: Bind off 5 sts, knit across: 29 sts.
Row 3: Work in K1, P1 ribbing across to last st, K1.
Row 4: P1, work in K1, P1 ribbing across.
Rows 5-14: Repeat Rows 3 and 4, 5 times.
FINISHING
Step 1: Cut the yarn leaving an 18″ end. Thread a yarn needle with the end and separately slip each stitch from the knitting needle onto the yarn.
Step 2: Fold the slipper in half lengthwise with **right** sides together.
Step 3: Pull the yarn **very** tightly gathering all the stitches firmly together and catch the first and last stitches together to secure; do **not** cut yarn.
Step 4: Sew the instep from the toe to the top of the bound off stitches, catching one stitch from each side and being careful to match rows.
Step 5: Weave yarn under several stitches of the seam and cut close to work.
Step 6: Thread a yarn needle with a 16″ piece of yarn. Sew the Back seam from the top to the Stockinette Stitch lines and secure. Weave the yarn through each of the remaining 9 stitches; pull **very** tightly and secure.
Step 7: Weave in all yarn ends.
Optional: Add pom-poms *(see Pom-pom, page 24)*.

Photograph on page 36.

Child Size:	4	6	8	10	12	14
Finished Measurement:	22″	23½″	25″	27″	29″	31″

Adult Size:	32	34	36	38	40
Finished Measurement:	32″	34″	36″	38″	40″

Size Note: Instructions are written for Child sizes in first parentheses with Adult sizes in second parentheses. Instructions will be easier to read, if you circle all the numbers pertaining to your size.

MATERIALS

Worsted Weight Yarn, approximately:
Main Color
 (2½-2½-3-3½-4-4½)(5½-6-6-6½-7) ounces,
 [(70-70-90-100-110-130)(160-170-170-180-200) grams,
 (160-160-190-220-250-280)(345-375-375-410-440) yards]
Contrasting Color
 (1½-2-2½-2½-3-3½)(4-4½-5-5-5½) ounces,
 [(40-60-70-70-90-100)(110-130-140-140-160) grams,
 (95-125-160-160-190-220)(250-280-315-315-345) yards]
Straight knitting needles, sizes 6 (4.25 mm) **and**
 8 (5.00 mm) **or** sizes needed for gauge
Crochet hook, size H (5.00 mm)
Buttons - (4)(6)
Yarn needle

GAUGE: With larger size needles, in Garter Stitch,
 18 sts and 34 rows (17 ridges) = 4″

MC STRIP

With larger size needles and MC, cast on
(24-26-28-30-32-34)(36-38-40-42-44) sts **loosely**.
Row 1 (Right side): With yarn in **front**, slip 1 as if to **purl**, knit across.
Note: Loop a short piece of yarn around any stitch to mark last row as **right** side.
Repeat Row 1 until Strip measures approximately
(18-20-22-24-26-28)(32-33-34-35-36)″ from cast on edge, ending by working a **wrong** side row.
Bind off all sts **loosely**.

CC STRIP

Using CC, work same as MC Strip.

With **right** sides facing, lay Strips side by side with the **cast on edge** of the MC Strip at bottom right and the **bound off edge** of the CC Strip at bottom left.
Place a marker on the inside edge of **each** Strip (19-21-23-26-28-30)(34-35-36-37-38) ridges up from bottom edge (Front) and down from top edge (Back).

JOINING

Beginning at Front markers and working in front loop only of each Slipped St, insert a crochet hook into first loop on the MC Strip **(Fig. 55a)**, insert hook into first loop on CC Strip and pull it through the MC loop **(Fig. 55b)**, ★ insert hook into next loop on MC Strip and pull it through CC loop, insert hook into next loop on CC Strip and pull it through MC loop; repeat from ★ to bottom edge of piece, ending by pulling yarn end through last loop on hook; secure end.
Repeat for Back.

Fig. 55a

Fig. 55b

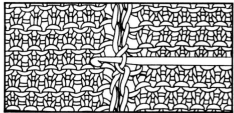

RIBBING

With smaller size needles and MC,
cast on 6 sts **loosely** (Tab); with **right** side facing,
pick up (48-52-56-60-64-68)(72-76-80-84-88) sts evenly spaced across bottom edge **(Fig. 42a, page 23)**; turn,
cast on 6 sts **(see Casting On, page 3)** (Tab):
(60-64-68-72-76-80)(84-88-92-96-100) sts.
Work in K1, P1 ribbing for (2)(3)″, ending by working a **wrong** side row.
Bind off all sts **loosely** in ribbing.
Repeat for second side.

With Front Tabs overlapping Back Tabs and working through **both** thicknesses, sew (2)(3) buttons on each side.
Weave in all yarn ends.

PULLOVER
Instructions on page 41

39

BABY AFGHAN
Instructions on page 42

BACK

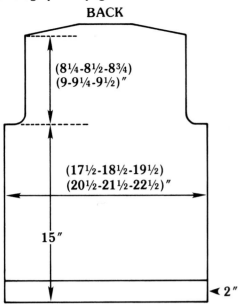

(8¼-8½-8¾)
(9-9¼-9½)″

(17½-18½-19½)
(20½-21½-22½)″

15″

◄ 2″

FRONT

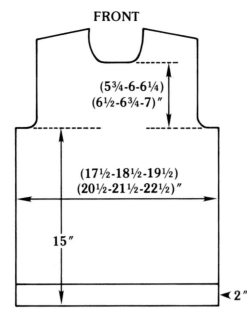

(5¾-6-6¼)
(6½-6¾-7)″

(17½-18½-19½)
(20½-21½-22½)″

15″

◄ 2″

SLEEVE

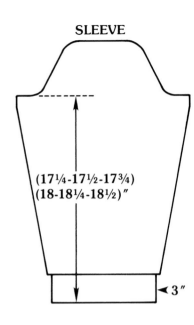

(17¼-17½-17¾)
(18-18¼-18½)″

◄ 3″

All measurements are approximate.

Size:	32	34	36	38	40	42
Finished Measurement:	35″	37″	39″	41″	43″	45″

Size Note: Instructions are written for sizes 32, 34, and 36 in first parentheses with sizes 38, 40, and 42 in second parentheses. Instructions will be easier to read, if you circle all the numbers pertaining to your size.

MATERIALS

Worsted Weight Yarn, approximately:
(16-17-18)(18½-19½-20½) ounces,
[(450-480-510)(520-550-580) grams,
(1,010-1,070-1,135)(1,165-1,225-1,290) yards]
Straight knitting needles, sizes 5 (3.75 mm) **and**
7 (4.50 mm) **or** sizes needed for gauge
16″ Circular needle, size 5 (3.75 mm)
2 Stitch holders
Marker
Yarn needle

GAUGE: With larger size needles, in Stockinette Stitch,
20 sts and 26 rows = 4″

BACK

RIBBING

With smaller size needles,
cast on (90-96-100)(106-110-116) sts **loosely.**
Work in K1, P1 ribbing for 2″.

BODY

Change to larger size needles.
Work in Stockinette Stitch (knit one row, purl one row) until Back measures approximately 15″ from cast on edge, ending by working a **purl** row.

Armhole Shaping

Rows 1 and 2: Bind off (5-6-6)(7-8-9) sts at the beginning of the next 2 rows, work across: (80-84-88)(92-94-98) sts.
Row 3 (Decrease row): Slip 1 as if to **knit**, K1, PSSO, knit across to last 2 sts, K2 tog: (78-82-86)(90-92-96) sts.
Row 4: Purl across.
Repeat Rows 3 and 4, (6-7-8)(9-8-9) times: (66-68-70)(72-76-78) sts.

Work even until Armholes measure approximately (8¼-8½-8¾)(9-9¼-9½)″, ending by working a **knit** row.

Shoulder Shaping

Rows 1 and 2: Bind off (6-6-6)(6-7-7) sts at the beginning of the next 2 rows, work across: (54-56-58)(60-62-64) sts.
Rows 3 and 4: Bind off (6-7-7)(7-7-7) sts at the beginning of the next 2 rows, work across: (42-42-44)(46-48-50) sts.
Rows 5 and 6: Bind off (7-7-7)(7-7-8) sts at the beginning of the next 2 rows, work across: (28-28-30)(32-34-34) sts.
Slip remaining sts onto st holder; cut yarn.

FRONT

Work same as Back until Armholes measure approximately (5¾-6-6¼)(6½-6¾-7)″, ending by working a **purl** row: (66-68-70)(72-76-78) sts.

Neck Shaping

Row 1: K(42-44-45)(47-49-51), slip (18-20-20)(22-22-24) sts just worked onto st holder, knit across: (24-24-25)(25-27-27) sts each side.
Note: Both sides of Neck are worked at the same time, using separate yarn for each side.
Row 2 (Decrease row): Purl across to within 2 sts of Neck edge, P2 tog; with second yarn, P2 tog, purl across: (23-23-24)(24-26-26) sts **each** side.
Row 3: Knit across to within 2 sts of Neck edge, K2 tog; with second yarn, slip 1 as if to **knit**, K1, PSSO, knit across: (22-22-23)(23-25-25) sts **each** side.
Row 4: Repeat Row 2: (21-21-22)(22-24-24) sts **each** side.
Row 5: Knit across; with second yarn, knit across.
Continue to decrease one stitch at **each** Neck edge, every other row, (2-1-2)(2-3-2) times **more**: (19-20-20)(20-21-22) sts **each** side.
Work even until Armholes measure same as Back to Shoulder Shaping, ending by working a **knit** row.

Shoulder Shaping

Rows 1 and 2: Bind off (6-6-6)(6-7-7) sts at the beginning of the next 2 rows, work across: (13-14-14)(14-14-15) sts **each** side.
Rows 3 and 4: Bind off (6-7-7)(7-7-7) sts at the beginning of the next 2 rows, work across: (7-7-7)(7-7-8) sts **each** side.
Row 5: Bind off (7-7-7)(7-7-8) sts; work across.
Bind off remaining sts.

41

SLEEVE (Make 2)

RIBBING

With smaller size needles,
cast on (42-46-48)(48-50-50) sts **loosely**.
Work in K1, P1 ribbing for 3" increasing 6 sts evenly spaced
across last row: (48-52-54)(54-56-56) sts.

BODY

Change to larger size needles.
Beginning with a **knit** row, work (6-8-8)(6-6-6) rows in
Stockinette Stitch.
Note: Increases are made by knitting into the front **and** into
the back of the same stitch.
Increase Row: Increase, knit across to last st, increase:
(50-54-56)(56-58-58) sts.
Continue to increase one stitch at **each** edge, every
(6-8-8)(6-6-6) rows, (1-5-4)(2-1-5) times **more**; then increase
every (8-10-10)(8-8-8) rows, (8-3-4)(8-9-6) times:
(68-70-72)(76-78-80) sts.
Work even until Sleeve measures approximately
(17¼-17½-17¾)(18-18¼-18½)" from cast on edge, ending
by working a **purl** row.

Sleeve Cap

Rows 1 and 2: Bind off (5-6-6)(7-8-9) sts at the beginning of
the next 2 rows, work across: (58-58-60)(62-62-62) sts.
Row 3 (Decrease row): Slip 1 as if to **knit**, K1, PSSO, knit
across to last 2 sts, K2 tog: (56-56-58)(60-60-60) sts.
Row 4: Purl across.
Repeat Rows 3 and 4, (13-14-15)(15-16-18) times:
(30-28-28)(30-28-24) sts.
Bind off 3 sts at the beginning of the next (4-6-6)(4-6-2) rows,
work across: (18-10-10)(18-10-18) sts.
Bind off 4 sts at the beginning of the next (2-0-0)(2-0-2) rows,
work across: 10 sts.
Bind off remaining sts.

FINISHING

Sew shoulder seams.

NECK RIBBING

With **right** side facing and using circular needle,
knit (28-28-30)(32-34-34) sts from Back st holder,
pick up 16 sts along left Front edge **(Fig. 42b, page 23)**,
knit (18-20-20)(22-22-24) sts from Front st holder,
pick up 16 sts along right Front edge, place marker:
(78-80-82)(86-88-90) sts.
Work in K1, P1 ribbing around for 1".
Bind off all sts **loosely** in ribbing.

Set in Sleeves matching center to shoulder seam.
Weave underarm and side in one continuous seam **(Fig. 37, page 22)**.
Weave in all yarn ends.

BABY AFGHAN

Photograph on page 40.

Finished Size: Approximately 33" x 42"

MATERIALS

Worsted Weight Yarn, approximately:
Main Color - 9½ ounces, (270 grams, 625 yards)
Color A - 6½ ounces, (180 grams, 430 yards)
Color B - 6½ ounces, (180 grams, 430 yards)
Straight knitting needles, size 7 (4.50 mm) **or** size
needed for gauge
Cable needle
Yarn needle

GAUGE: One Panel (33 sts) = 4¾"

PANEL

Make 3 using MC; make 2 **each** using Color A and Color B.
Note: Increases are made by knitting into the front **and** into
the back of the same stitch.
Cast on 33 sts **loosely**.
Row 1 (Right side): P2, K6, P2, increase in next st,
K4, [slip 1 as if to **knit**, K2 tog, PSSO **(a two stitch
decrease)**], K3, increase in next st, K1, P2, K6, P2.
Row 2: K2, P6, K2, P 13, K2, P6, K2.
Row 3: P2, [slip next 3 sts onto cable needle and hold in
front of work, K3, K3 from cable needle **(Front Cable
made)**], P2, increase in next st, K4, slip 1 as if to **knit**,
K2 tog, PSSO, K3, increase in next st, K1, P2, [slip next 3 sts
onto cable needle and hold in **back** of work, K3, K3 from
cable needle **(Back Cable made)**], P2.
Row 4: K2, P6, K 17, P6, K2.
Rows 5-7: Repeat Rows 1 and 2 once, then repeat Row 1
once **more**.
Row 8: K2, P6, K 17, P6, K2.
Repeat Rows 1-8 for pattern until Panel measures
approximately 42" from cast on edge, ending by working
Row 8.
Bind off all sts **loosely** in pattern.

FINISHING

Lay out Panels in the following order:
A, MC, B, MC, B, MC, A.
Weave Panels together **(Fig. 38, page 22)**.
Weave in all yarn ends.

43

HOODED BABY JACKET
Instructions on page 47

44

SAMPLER VEST

Photograph on page 43.

"Once you have mastered the basics, the Sampler Vest combines many of the techniques taught in this leaflet; plus, it features something new - Smocking!"

BACK & FRONT

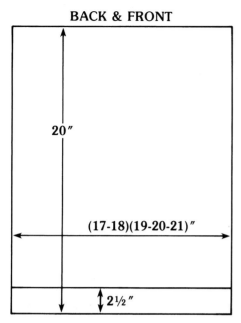

20"

(17-18)(19-20-21)"

2½"

All measurements are approximate.

Size:	32	34	36	38	40
Finished Measurement:	34"	36"	38"	40"	42"

Size Note: Instructions are written for sizes 32 and 34 in first parentheses with sizes 36, 38, and 40 in second parentheses. Instructions will be easier to read, if you circle all the numbers pertaining to your size.

MATERIALS
Worsted Weight Yarn, approximately:
Main Color - (9-9½)(10-10½-11) ounces,
[(260-270)(280-300-310) grams,
(570-600)(630-660-690) yards]
Contrasting Color - 1 ounce, (30 grams, 65 yards)
Straight knitting needles, sizes 5 (3.75 mm) **and**
7 (4.50 mm) **or** sizes needed for gauge
Cable needle
Markers
Yarn needle

GAUGE: With larger size needles, in Stockinette Stitch,
20 sts and 26 rows = 4"

Note: Row gauge is very important in this design
(see Row Gauge, page 30).

BACK

RIBBING
With MC and smaller size needles,
cast on (87-93)(97-103-107) sts **loosely.**
Row 1: K5 (Garter Stitch Border), P1, (K1, P1) across to last 5 sts, K5 (Garter Stitch Border).
Row 2: K6, P1, (K1, P1) across to last 6 sts, K6.
Rows 3-19: Repeat Rows 1 and 2, 8 times; then repeat Row 1 once **more.**

CABLE PANEL
Change to larger size needles.
Row 1 (Right side): K5, place marker, P2 tog (1-0)(1-0-1) time, P(10-13)(12-15-14), K6, ★ P(10-11)(12-13-14), K6; repeat from ★ 2 times **more,** P(11-13)(13-15-15), place marker, K5: (86-93)(96-103-106) sts.
Row 2: K(16-18)(18-20-20), P6, ★ K(10-11)(12-13-14), P6; repeat from ★ 2 times **more,** knit across.
Row 3: K5, P(11-13)(13-15-15), [slip next 3 sts onto cable needle and hold in **back** of work, K3, K3 from cable needle **(Cable made)**], ★ P(10-11)(12-13-14), work Cable; repeat from ★ 2 times **more,** purl to marker, K5.
Row 4: Repeat Row 2.
Row 5: K5, P(11-13)(13-15-15), K6, ★ P(10-11)(12-13-14), K6; repeat from ★ 2 times **more,** purl to marker, K5.
Row 6: Repeat Row 2.
Row 7: Repeat Row 5.
Rows 8-28: Repeat Rows 2-7, 3 times; then repeat Rows 2-4 once **more.**
Row 29: Knit across decreasing (8-9)(8-9-8) sts evenly spaced between markers: (78-84)(88-94-98) sts.
Rows 30-32: Knit across.

HEART PANEL
Row 1: Knit across.
Row 2: K5, purl to marker, K5.
Rows 3-22: Repeat Rows 1 and 2, 10 times.
Row 23: K5, K2 tog, knit across: (77-83)(87-93-97) sts.
Rows 24-26: Knit across.

LACE PANEL
Row 1: K6, ★ YO *(Fig. 30a, page 13)*, SSK *(Figs. 15a-c, page 10)*; repeat from ★ across to marker, K5.
Rows 2-4: K5, purl to marker, K5.
Rows 5-26: Repeat Rows 1-4, 5 times; then repeat Rows 1 and 2 once **more.**
Row 27: Knit across increasing (10-8)(8-10-10) sts evenly spaced: (87-91)(95-103-107) sts.
Rows 28-30: Knit across.

SMOCKED PANEL
Row 1: K6, P3, (K1, P3) across to last 6 sts, K6.
Row 2: K5, P1, (K3, P1) across to marker, K5.
Rows 3-24: Repeat Rows 1 and 2, 11 times.

SHOULDER RIBBING
Row 1: K6, P1, (K1, P1) across to last 6 sts, K6.
Row 2: K5, P1, (K1, P1) across to last 5 sts, K5.
Rows 3-8: Repeat Rows 1 and 2, 3 times.
Bind off all sts in pattern.

FRONT
Work same as Back.

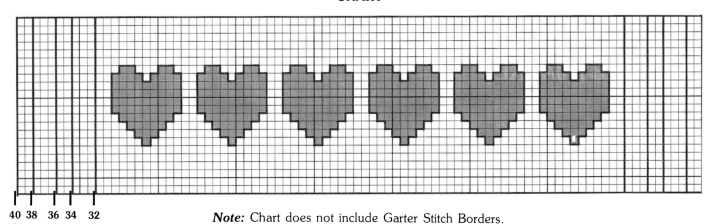

40 38 36 34 32
└─SIZES─┘

Note: Chart does not include Garter Stitch Borders.

FINISHING

HEARTS

With CC work Duplicate Stitch on Heart Panel
(Figs. 43a & 43b, page 23) following Chart.

SMOCKING

With **right** side of Back facing, using CC, and beginning at
lower left edge of Smocked Panel, bring yarn up at left of
fifth stitch of first vertical line *(Point A, Fig. 56a)*. Insert
needle from right to left through corresponding stitch on next
line *(Point B, Fig. 56a)*, then through first stitch, pulling yarn
until lines meet (not **too** tightly). Stitch again over same stitch,
then pull the yarn to the wrong side at Point B.
Bring yarn up at left of tenth stitch of second vertical line
(Point C, Fig. 56b). Insert needle from right to left through
corresponding stitch on next line *(Point D, Fig. 56b)*, then
through first stitch, pulling yarn until lines meet. Stitch again
over same stitch, pulling yarn to the wrong side at Point D.
Bring yarn up at left of fifth stitch of third vertical line
(Point E, Fig. 56b).
Repeat this process across working through fifth and tenth
stitches of vertical lines; then repeat working through fifteenth
and twentieth stitches of vertical lines.
Repeat on Front.

Sew shoulder seams, leaving a 9″ Neck opening.
Weave side seams *(Fig. 38, page 22)*, leaving Lace Panel
open for Armholes.
Weave in all yarn ends.

Fig. 56a

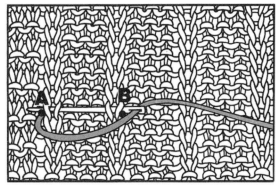

Fig. 56b

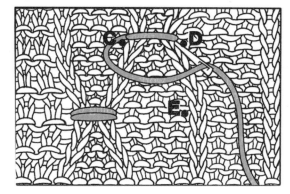

"Okay, now you're ready for a challenge. You've made a dozen pairs of Slippers, you've breezed through the basic pullover, and the Sampler Vest just looked difficult (but you discovered that it really wasn't). Besides, baby garments are such fun to knit. This little jacket does require some experience - please don't attempt it without first knitting some of the more basic designs."

HOODED BABY JACKET

Photograph on page 44.

Size:	1	2	4
Chest Measurement:	20″	21″	22″
Finished Measurement:	22″	23″	24″

Size Note: Instructions are written for size 1 with sizes 2 and 4 in parentheses. Instructions will be easier to read, if you circle all the numbers pertaining to your size.

MATERIALS
    Worsted Weight Yarn, approximately:
        7(8½-10) ounces, [200(240-280) grams,
        460(560-655) yards]
    Straight knitting needles, sizes 5 (3.75 mm) **and**
      7 (4.50 mm) **or** sizes needed for gauge
    24″ Circular needle, size 7 (4.50 mm)
    Cable needle
    4 Stitch holders
    Markers
    12(12-14)″ Jacket zipper
    Sewing needle and thread
    Yarn needle

GAUGE: With larger size needles, in Stockinette Stitch,
       20 sts and 26 rows = 4″

BACK

RIBBING
With smaller size needles, cast on 58(60-62) sts **loosely**.
Work in K1, P1 ribbing for 7 rows.
BODY
Change to larger size needles.
Beginning with a **knit** row, work in Stockinette Stitch (knit one row, purl one row) until Back measures approximately 7½(8½-9½)″ from cast on edge, ending by working a **purl** row.
Armhole Shaping
Row 1 (Right side): Bind off 2 sts, knit across: 56(58-60) sts.
Row 2: Bind off 2 sts, purl across: 54(56-58) sts.
Cut yarn leaving a 4″ end.
Slip remaining sts onto st holder.

SLEEVE (Make 2)

RIBBING
With smaller size needles, cast on 30(32-36) sts **loosely**.
Work in K1, P1 ribbing for 11 rows.
BODY
Change to larger size needles.
Row 1 (Right side): Knit across.
Row 2: Purl across.
Note: Increases are worked by knitting into the front **and** into the back of the same stitch.
Row 3 (Increase row): Increase, knit across to last st, increase: 32(34-38) sts.
Continue to work in Stockinette Stitch increasing one stitch at **each** edge, every 6(8-10) rows, 5 times: 42(44-48) sts.
Work even until Sleeve measures approximately 7(9-10½)″ from cast on edge, ending by working a **purl** row.
Shaping
Row 1: Bind off 2 sts, knit across: 40(42-46) sts.
Row 2: Bind off 2 sts, purl across: 38(40-44) sts.
Cut yarn leaving a 4″ end.
Slip remaining sts onto st holder.

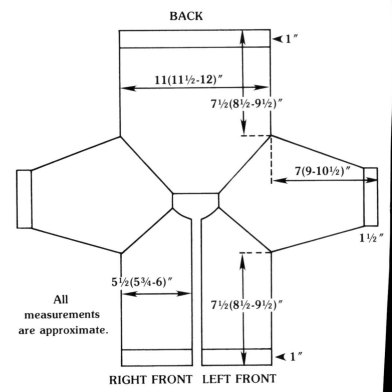

BACK

◄1″

11(11½-12)″

7½(8½-9½)″

7(9-10½)″

1½″

5½(5¾-6)″

All measurements are approximate.

7½(8½-9½)″

◄1″

RIGHT FRONT   LEFT FRONT

CABLE PATTERN (6 sts)
Row 1 (Right side): P1, K4, P1.
Row 2: K1, P4, K1.
Row 3: P1, [slip next 2 sts onto cable needle and hold in **back** of work, K2, K2 sts from cable needle **(Cable made)**], P1.
Row 4: K1, P4, K1.
Repeat Rows 1-4 for pattern.

LEFT FRONT

RIBBING
With smaller size needles, cast on 30(32-34) sts **loosely**.
Row 1: K2, (P1, K1) across.
Row 2: P1, (K1, P1) across to last 3 sts, K3.
Rows 3-7: Repeat Rows 1 and 2 twice, then repeat Row 1 once **more**.
BODY
Change to larger size needles.
Row 1 (Right side): K 21(23-25), place marker, work Row 1 of Cable Pattern, K3.
Row 2: K2, P1, work next row of Cable Pattern, purl across.
Row 3: Knit to marker, work next row of Cable Pattern, K3.
Repeat Rows 2 and 3 for pattern until piece measures approximately 7½(8½-9½)″ from cast on edge, ending by working Cable Pattern Row 2.
Armhole Shaping
Row 1: Bind off 2 sts, knit to marker, work next row of Cable Pattern, K3: 28(30-32) sts.
Row 2: K2, P1, work next row of Cable Pattern, purl across.
Cut yarn leaving a 4″ end.
Slip remaining sts onto st holder.

RIGHT FRONT

RIBBING
With smaller size needles, cast on 30(32-34) sts **loosely**.
Row 1: (K1, P1) across to last 2 sts, K2.
Row 2: K3, P1, (K1, P1) across.
Rows 3-7: Repeat Rows 1 and 2 twice, then repeat Row 1 once **more**.

BODY

Change to larger size needles.

Row 1 (Right side): K3, work Row 1 of Cable Pattern, place marker, knit across.

Row 2: Purl to marker, work next row of Cable Pattern, P1, K2.

Row 3: K3, work next row of Cable Pattern, knit across.

Repeat Rows 2 and 3 for pattern until piece measures approximately 7½(8½-9½)″ from cast on edge, ending by working Cable Pattern Row 3.

Armhole Shaping

Row 1: Bind off 2 sts, purl to marker, work next row of Cable Pattern, P1, K2; do **not** cut yarn: 28(30-32) sts.

YOKE

With **wrong** side facing, slip sts from all st holders onto circular needle as follows: Left Front, Sleeve, Back, Sleeve, Right Front: 186(196-210) sts.

Row 1: Beginning at Right Front, K3, work Row 1 of Cable Pattern, K 14(16-18), K2 tog, place marker, work Row 1 of Cable Pattern, place marker, SSK *(Figs. 15a-c, page 10)*, K 28(30-34), K2 tog, place marker, work Row 1 of Cable Pattern, place marker, SSK, K 44(46-48), K2 tog, place marker, work Row 1 of Cable Pattern, place marker, SSK, K 28(30-34), K2 tog, place marker, work Row 1 of Cable Pattern, place marker, SSK, K 14(16-18), work Row 1 of Cable Pattern, K3: 178(188-202) sts.

Row 2: K2, P1, work next row of Cable Pattern, ★ purl to marker, work next row of Cable Pattern; repeat from ★ across to last 3 sts, P1, K2.

Row 3: K3, work next row of Cable Pattern, ★ knit to marker, work next row of Cable Pattern; repeat from ★ across to last 3 sts, K3.

Row 4: K2, P1, work next row of Cable Pattern, ★ purl to marker, work next row of Cable Pattern; repeat from ★ across to last 3 sts, P1, K2.

Row 5 (Decrease row): K3, work next row of Cable Pattern, ★ knit to within 2 sts of marker, K2 tog, work next row of Cable Pattern, SSK; repeat from ★ 3 times **more**, knit to marker, work next row of Cable Pattern, K3: 170(180-194) sts.

Repeat Rows 2-5, 0(1-2) times: 170(172-178) sts.

Repeat Rows 4 and 5, 10 times; then repeat Row 4 once **more**: 90(92-98) sts.

Neck Shaping

Row 1: K3, P1, slip 4 sts just worked onto st holder, work Cable, P1, ★ knit to within 2 sts of marker, K2 tog, work next row of Cable Pattern, SSK; repeat from ★ 3 times **more**, knit to marker, work next row of Cable Pattern, K3: 78(80-86) sts.

Row 2: K2, P1, K1, slip 4 sts just worked onto st holder, P4, K1, purl to marker, ★ work next row of Cable Pattern, purl to marker; repeat from ★ across to last 5 sts, K1, P4: 74(76-82) sts.

Row 3: SSK, K2, P1, ★ knit to within 2 sts of marker, K2 tog, work next row of Cable Pattern, SSK; repeat from ★ 3 times **more**, knit to marker, P1, K2, K2 tog: 64(66-72) sts.

Row 4: P3, K1, purl to marker, ★ work next row of Cable Pattern, purl to marker; repeat from ★ across to last 4 sts, K1, P3.

Row 5: SSK, K1, P1, K 0(1-2), † K2 tog, work next row of Cable Pattern, SSK, K 0(0-2), K2 tog, work next row of Cable Pattern, SSK †, knit to within 2 sts of marker, repeat from † to † once, K 0(1-2), P1, K1, K2 tog: 54(56-62) sts.

Row 6: P2, K1, P1(2-3), † work next row of Cable Pattern, P2(2-4), work next row of Cable Pattern †, purl to marker, repeat from † to † once, P1(2-3), K1, P2.

Size 1 ONLY:

Row 7: SSK, K2 tog, (work next row of Cable Pattern, SSK) twice, knit to within 2 sts of marker, K2 tog, (work next row of Cable Pattern, SSK) twice, K2 tog: 46 sts.

Row 8: P2, K1, P4, K2 tog, K1, P4, K1, purl to marker, K1, P4, K1, K2 tog, P4, K1, P2, remove markers: 44 sts.

Row 9: SSK, P2 tog, K3, P2 tog, work Cable, P1, SSK, K 12, K2 tog, P1, work Cable, P2 tog, K3, P2 tog, K2 tog: 36 sts.

Row 10: P1, K1, P3, K1, P4, K1, P 14, K1, P4, K1, P3, K1, P1; cut yarn.

Size 2 ONLY:

Row 7: SSK, P1, K2 tog, (work next row of Cable Pattern, SSK) twice, knit to within 2 sts of marker, K2 tog, (work next row of Cable Pattern, SSK) twice, P1, K2 tog: 48 sts.

Row 8: (P1, K1) twice, P4, K2 tog, K1, P4, K1, purl to marker, K1, P4, K1, K2 tog, P4, (K1, P1) twice, remove markers: 46 sts.

Row 9: SSK, (P2 tog, work Cable) twice, P1, SSK, K 12, K2 tog, P1, (work Cable, P2 tog) twice, K2 tog: 38 sts.

Row 10: P1, K1, (P4, K1) twice, P 14, K1, (P4, K1) twice, P1; cut yarn.

Size 4 ONLY:

Row 7: SSK, P1, K1, (K2 tog, work next row of Cable Pattern, SSK) twice, knit to within 2 sts of marker, (K2 tog, work next row of Cable Pattern, SSK) twice, K1, P1, K2 tog: 52 sts.

Row 8: P1, K1, (P2, K1, P4, K1) twice, purl to marker, (K1, P4, K1, P2) twice, K1, P1, remove markers.

Row 9: SSK, K2 tog, P1, work Cable, P2 tog twice, work Cable, P1, SSK, K 12, K2 tog, P1, work Cable, P2 tog twice, work Cable, P1, SSK, K2 tog: 42 sts.

Row 10: P2, K1, P4, K2 tog, P4, K1, P 14, K1, P4, K2 tog, P4, K1, P2; cut yarn: 40 sts.

FINISHING

NECK BAND

With **right** side facing and smaller size needles, (K3, P1) from Right Front st holder, pick up 10 sts along Right Neck edge, K 36(38-40) from circular needle, pick up 11 sts along Left Neck edge, (P1, K3) from Left Front st holder: 65(67-69) sts.

Row 1 (Wrong side): K2, P1, (K1, P1) across to last 2 sts, K2.

Row 2: K3, P1, (K1, P1) across to last 3 sts, K3.

Rows 3-7: Repeat Rows 1 and 2 twice, then repeat Row 1 once **more**.

HOOD

Change to larger size needles.

Row 1 (Right side): K3, work Row 1 of Cable Pattern, place marker, K 22(23-24), increase in next st, place marker, increase in next st, knit across to last 9 sts, place marker, work Row 1 of Cable Pattern, K3: 67(69-71) sts.

Row 2: K2, P1, work next row of Cable Pattern, purl to last marker, work next row of Cable Pattern, P1, K2.

Row 3: K3, work next row of Cable Pattern, knit to last marker, work next row of Cable Pattern, K3.

Rows 4-8: Repeat Rows 2 and 3 twice, then repeat Row 2 once **more**.

Row 9 (Increase row): K3, work next row of Cable Pattern, knit to within one st of marker, increase in next 2 sts, knit to marker, work next row of Cable Pattern, K3: 69(71-73) sts.

Rows 10-41: Repeat Rows 2-9, 4 times **more**: 77(79-81) sts.

Work even until Hood measures approximately 8¼(8¾-9¼)″ from Neck Band, ending by working a **wrong** side row.

Bind off all sts in pattern.

Weave underarm and side in one continuous seam *(Fig. 37, page 22)*.

Fold bound off edge at top of Hood in half and backstitch this seam.

Sew in zipper, starting at bottom of Jacket.

Weave in all yarn ends.

48

INDEX